THE SURVIVAL OF SMALL BUSINESSES IN NORTHEASTERN FLORIDA AFTER A NATURAL DISASTER

DR. HARRY KEMP

"Dr. Kemp is a Quantitative Analyst and Business Consultant specializing in reviewing, analyzing and enhancing internal company programs and initiatives to improve performance. He is a graduate of Walden University, and earned a Doctorate of Business Administration (DBA) with a concentration in Leadership. He has 25 years of business administration experience as well as a diverse set of skills in Leadership, Project Management, Business Process Analysis, Program Assessment & Improvement, Policy Implementation and Department & Division Management. As a retired Fire-Rescue Captain, Dr. Kemp has expertly trained, coordinated and managed team members to ensure timely and safe responses to emergency and non-emergency situations. With a Masters of Business Administration (MBA) and a Bachelor's of Science (BSA) accompanied by a concentration in Organizational Management, he offers a varied educational background in areas of business and management. Dr. Kemp's current doctoral study, The Survival of Small Businesses in Northeastern Florida After a Natural Disaster, earned him the 2017 Frank Dilley Award for Outstanding Doctoral Study."

Walden University

College of Management and Technology

This is to certify that the doctoral study by

Harry Kemp

has been found to be complete and satisfactory in all respects,
and that any and all revisions required by
the review committee have been made.

Review Committee
Dr. Marilyn Simon, Committee Chairperson, Doctor of Business Administration Faculty

Dr. William Stokes, Committee Member, Doctor of Business Administration Faculty

Dr. Patricia Fusch, University Reviewer, Doctor of Business Administration Faculty

Chief Academic Officer
Eric Riedel, Ph.D.

Walden University
2016

Abstract

The Survival of Small Businesses in Northeastern Florida After a Natural Disaster

by

Harry A. Kemp

MS, Jacksonville University, 2003

BS, Edward Waters College, 1999

Doctoral Study Submitted in Partial Fulfillment

of the Requirements for the Degree of

Doctor of Business Administration

Walden University

December 2016

Abstract

Many small business owners lack strategies needed to prevent permanent business closure in the wake of extreme natural disaster situations. After a natural disaster, small businesses suffer financial losses in millions of dollars related to damage and destruction that disrupt their lives, families, and communities. This multiple case study explored strategies that 5 small business owners in northeastern Florida used to avoid permanent business closure in the aftermath of a natural disaster. The theory of planned behavior and vested interest theory were the conceptual frameworks used in this multiple case study. In–depth interviews with purposively selected small business owners were supplemented with a review of documentation from archival records. Yin's 5-step analysis guided the coding process of participants' responses, and member checking was used to validate the transcribed data. The major themes of the study revealed the owners' strategies relating to flood barriers, maintaining adequate insurance coverage, damage and destruction aftermath, and experience with natural disasters. This study's implications for social change include contributing to social stability and continuing economic growth by benefitting small business owners without a natural disaster plan or a plan that needs updating, new small business owners, and community organizations. This study may benefit small businesses by providing lessons learned on how to survive natural disasters.

The Survival of Small Businesses in Northeastern Florida After a Natural Disaster

by

Harry A. Kemp

MS, Jacksonville University, 2003

BS, Edward Waters College, 1999

Doctoral Study Submitted in Partial Fulfillment

of the Requirements for the Degree of

Doctor of Business Administration

Walden University

December 2016

Dedication

This study is dedicated to God, who is the head of my life. I also dedicate this study to

my sons, Keino and Omari, you can do anything through Christ. Lastly, in memory of my

late mother, Cassie McCoy, and father, Lee Kemp, thank you for believing. Also, I would

like to dedicate this study to all of the people who encouraged me to pursue this

endeavor.

Acknowledgments

Special thanks to Dr. Marilyn Simon for her unwavering support throughout this journey. Dr. Simon provided unbelievable mentoring, especially during the times when I was at my lowest point of this process. I believe divine intervention allowed me to work with this great mentor. Dr. Simon is that beacon of light that every doctoral student and candidate needs during this marathon.

I would also like to thank Dr. William Stokes, my second committee member, for his additional support and guidance. Dr. Stokes provided additional feedback that increased the quality of my study. Also, some special thanks go out to Dr. Patricia Fusch (URR) for her detailed peer-review focus. Special thanks to Dr. Freda Turner for her encouragement and belief that I would complete this program. Thanks to my APA coach, Toni Williams, for her constant feedback and eye for detail. I also would like to thank all of my friends for taking the time out of their busy schedules to read and make scholarly suggestions that could improve my study.

Table of Contents

Section 1: Foundation of the Study

Business owners must plan and prepare for natural disasters to avoid consequent business closures (Sadiq & Tyler, 2016), but small business owners prepare less for natural disasters when compared to owners of large corporations (Levy, Yu, & Prizzia, 2016). Hurricane Katrina was one of the costliest natural disasters in U.S. history, as relief efforts totaled an estimated $73.8 billion (Xu & Lu, 2013). Despite record–breaking costs in repairs and structural damage among small businesses, only 15% of small business owners prepare for natural disasters compared to 45% of large businesses (Sarmiento et al., 2015). In addition to a company's size, knowledge of survival techniques and industry sector types (Levy et al., 2016; Sadiq & Graham, 2015) play a major role in surviving natural disasters. Consequently, a comprehensive lens is necessary for analysis to ensure business continuity during and after a natural disaster (Sahebjamnia, Torabi, & Mansouri, 2015). Sharing the strategies acquired by small business owners who avoided business closure after a natural disaster may help other business owners prevent business failure in the aftermath of a natural disaster.

Background of the Problem

Natural disasters occur every year in the United States, cost millions of dollars in repairs, and disrupt the lives of many people. Between 1985 and 2009, floods accounted for most natural disasters around the world (Cunado & Ferreira, 2013). Cyclones and tornadoes were the major natural disaster between 1920 and 1940 (Boustan, Kahn, & Rhode, 2012). For this study, the definition of a small business was an independent business with fewer than 500 employees (U.S. Small Business Administration [SBA], 2014). Small businesses are affected by natural disasters in Florida every year.

Some businesses may never recover from the effects of a natural disaster because of the amount of economic destruction (Cunado & Ferreira, 2013). Business leaders of large industries and corporations are often able to maintain business continuity with strategies designed to be proactive (Asgary, Anjum, & Azimi, 2012; Patankar & Patwardhan, 2016). In contrast, only 22% of small business owners reported they could reopen after a natural disaster and operate at the predisaster level or better (Asgary et al., 2012; Federal Emergency Management Agency [FEMA], 2015b). Small business owners may be at greater risk of market failure following natural disasters, especially those without effective disaster strategies (FEMA, 2015b; Sahebjamnia et al., 2015). The next section will include more information on the severity of small business failure in the aftermath of natural disasters.

Problem Statement

Between 1995 and 2013, global natural disaster economic losses totaled $2 trillion (United Nations Office for Disaster Risk Reduction, 2013). Thousands of business owners temporarily or permanently close their doors in the aftermath of a natural disaster each year (Fischer-Smith, 2013). The general business problem is that some small business owners in the wholesale and retail industry encounter the negative effects of natural disasters that result in 40% of small businesses in the United States going out of business each year because of natural disasters (Schrank, Marshall, Hall-Phillips, Wiatt, & Jones, 2013). The specific business problem is that some small business owners in northeastern Florida lack strategies to avoid permanent business closure in the aftermath of a natural disaster.

Purpose Statement

The purpose of this qualitative multiple case study was to explore what strategies business owners in northeastern Florida have used to avoid permanent business closure in the aftermath of a natural disaster. The target population consisted of retail and wholesale small business owners in northeastern Florida who avoided permanent business closure in the aftermath of a natural disaster. The implications for positive social change include the potential for small business owners to address the potential for a natural disaster proactively, maintain employment, and continue to have a positive economic effect on their community.

Nature of the Study

As the researcher, I used the qualitative research method in this study. Research methods consist of three types: qualitative, quantitative, and mixed methods (Sonenshein, DeCelles, & Dutton, 2014; Taber, 2012). The quantitative research method involves collecting and analyzing numerical data to describe, explain, predict, or control the phenomenon of interest (Morse, 2015), which was not the focus of this research. Qualitative exploratory research involves using semistructured interview questions to gather detailed data that lead to open–ended responses (Morse, 2015; Steelman & McCaffrey, 2013; Taber, 2012). A semistructured interview protocol allows for repetition and allows participants the freedom to express their story within the parameters of the question (Morse, 2015; Stake, 2010). In this study, the semistructured questions led to a realistic interpretation of the lessons learned from the aftermath of a natural disaster. A mixed–methods study includes both quantitative and qualitative data collection and analysis (Anderson, Leahy, DelValle, Sherman, & Tansey, 2014), which was not appropriate for revealing the experiences business owners used to avoid permanent business closure in the aftermath of a natural disaster.

In this study, I used a qualitative multiple case study design. Researchers conduct case study research to interpret and describe event experiences and to develop an in–depth description of a problem and its solutions (Hancock & Algozzine, 2011; Yin, 2014). Multiple case study tactics provide interviewers with the freedom to explore (Stake, 2010) as opposed to an ethnographic design that has shared cultures as its focus (Leedy & Ormrod, 2013). In this study, the focus was on the strategies that small business leaders used to develop and execute preparedness and recovery plans successfully and thereby, prevent business closure.

Within a case study design, the focus is on a general situation in a real–life setting (Yin, 2014). As this was the focus of this study, other qualitative research designs were not suitable. For example, phenomenological studies involve looking at the lived experiences and the meaning of participants' experiences regarding a phenomenon (Abu-Qamar & Wilson, 2012; Giorgi, 2012; Skiba & Disch, 2014), which was not the intent of this study. The focus of grounded theory is to develop theories using empirical analysis to reinforce theory (Prior & Miller, 2012). This study did not have a focus on theory discovery, grounded theory, or ethnographic research (Hancock & Algozzine, 2011; Johnson, Buehring, Prior, & Miller, 2012). Instead, the focus of this study was on the strategies that small business leaders use to prepare for natural disasters and avoid business closures.

Research Question

This research question may impact change by providing business leaders with natural disaster success strategies that prevent business closure. Also, answers to the research question may prevent or reduce unemployment from natural disasters in their respective communities. The research question that guided this study was: What strategies do small business owners use to avoid permanent business closure in the aftermath of a natural disaster?

Interview Question

I used the following semistructured interview questions to collect data from participants who were able to explain their in–depth experiences with previous natural disasters:

1. What is your experience with planning for a natural disaster?
2. How have you, as a business owner in northeast Florida, avoided permanent business closure in the aftermath of a natural disaster?
3. What strategies did your business implement during the natural disaster you experienced?
4. What were the business norms, attitudes, and responses immediately following the natural disaster?
5. How did self-efficacy (confidence) in your procedure help your business in the aftermath of a natural disaster?

6. How much damage and destruction has a natural disaster caused to your

business?

7. Please elaborate on different strategies your business might enact to avoid

permanent business closure from a natural disaster?

Conceptual Frameworks

Two conceptual frameworks supported this qualitative multiple case study: the

theory of planned behavior (TPB) and vested interest (VI) theory. Ajzen (1985)

developed the TPB with the central idea that intentions and perceived control are the

foundations of behavioral antecedents (Ajzen & Klobas, 2013; Choi, 2012). In TPB,

Ajzen extended the theory of reasoned action because intent did not always result in

expected behavior, so Ajzen included perceived control, which includes a focus on a

person's perception of how much control that individual has over the behavioral outcome

(Choi, 2012). The tenets that formed the framework of this study included people's

intentions, norms, and controlled responses to natural disasters (Altay, Prasad, & Tata,

2013; Xin, Karamehic-Muratovic, & Cluphf, 2016). For example, TPB includes the

actions or inactions of individuals (Ajzen & Sheikh, 2013). Business leaders may use

TPB as a positive framework for understanding other leaders' planning decisions related

to catastrophic events (Mancha & Yoder, 2015; Wang & Ritchie, 2012). The TPB

conceptual framework was suitable for exploring how business leaders use emergency

plans for business continuity.

Crano first introduced VI theory in 1983 (De Dominicis et al., 2014) and

proposed that a person's stake or VI in a given attitude depend on the meaningfulness and timeliness of that person's perceived consequences (Miller, Adame, & Moore, 2013). The degree to which an individual feels vested in a particular outcome relates to the magnitude to which that outcome directly affects that individual (Johnson, Siegel, & Crano, 2014). The four attitudinal elements of the framework are: salience of attitude, perceived certainty of consequences, perceived immediacy or remoteness of consequences, and belief in a person's own ability to use attitude-relevant behaviors (Crano & Prislin, 1995). In this study, I used VI theory as a lens to help me understand why small business stakeholders should have a VI in disaster planning. The degree to which people participate in and support funding for disaster preparedness directly relates to how they perceive their personal risk (Miller et al., 2013). The VI conceptual framework served as a lens that business leaders can use to help stakeholders understand the risk natural disasters pose to their business, their employees, and the economy.

Operational Definitions

Business continuity planning: Business continuity planning is a way business leaders combine assets to formulate a plan to prevent business interruptions (Epstein & Khan, 2014).

Climate change adaptation: Climate change adaptation is the innovative actions that stop or limit the onset of anticipated extreme weather change risk from manmade or natural catastrophe changes in the atmosphere (Matzenberger, Hargreaves, Raha, & Dias, 2015).

Federal Emergency Management Agency (FEMA): FEMA is an independent organization formed in 1979 to organize responses to catastrophes in the United States (FEMA, 2015a).

Natural disasters: Events of catastrophic proportion that cause extreme environmental results, such as floods, tornadoes, hurricanes, volcanic eruptions, earthquakes, heat waves, and landslides (Lamanna, Williams, & Childers, 2012).

Saffir-Simpson Index: Scientists developed the Saffir-Simpson Hurricane Wind Scale based on wind effects and classifying hurricanes into five categories. The categories are: (a) Category 1 is 55–74 miles per hour (MPH), (b) Category 2 is 96–100 MPH, (c) Category 3 is 111–130 MPH, (d) Category 4 is 131–154 MPH, and (e) Category 5 is considered greater than 155 MPH (Blake, Landsea, & Gibney, 2007; FEMA, 2015b; National Oceanic and Atmospheric Administration [NOAA], 2016).

Assumptions, Limitations, and Delimitations

Assumptions

Assumptions are beliefs without supporting evidence (Leedy & Ormrod, 2013; Machi & McEvoy, 2012). Researchers provide their assumptions to establish truth in research (Kirkwood & Price, 2013). In this study, my primary assumption was that the small business owners who participated would be honest in their responses to how business owners avoid permanent business closure during the aftermath of a natural disaster. As participation was voluntary, meeting this assumption was likely. I also assumed that if managers and business leaders understood the link between business continuity and disaster planning more, small businesses could survive the aftermath of a natural disaster.

Limitations

A limitation refers to a researcher's biases toward the outcome of a study (Sarmiento et al., 2015). Limitations are uncontrolled elements that may influence study outcomes (Hancock & Algozzine, 2011). In this study, the small sample was one limitation, as well as the specific phenomenon analyzed, as it was unique to one large geographical area (Venkatesh, Brown, & Bala, 2013), and so, the research findings might not apply to broader populations. There were 25,000 businesses in the geographical area, but I limited this study to existing businesses affected by natural disasters in northeastern Florida.

Delimitations

A substantial portion of case study research is defining the delimitations or bounds of the investigation (Merriam & Tisdell, 2015). Delimitations are features of a study that a researcher chooses to set the scope and boundary of the study to answer the research question (Leedy & Ormrod, 2013; Venkatesh et al., 2013). I delimited the study to small businesses that continued to thrive after a natural disaster that hit northeastern Florida. Excluded from this study were any businesses with more than 500 employees.

Significance of the Study

The state of Florida is prone to more tropical cyclones than any other state in the United States (Villarini, Goska, Smith, & Vecchi, 2014). The goal of this study was to provide potential lessons learned about maintaining a business in the aftermath of a natural disaster to small business owners and to provide social change. During the hurricane season of 2012, Florida residents experienced Tropical Storm Beryl (Stewart, 2013). The case for this study was Tropical Storm Beryl. The recovery cost from this historic hurricane season was high, as the storms affected many small businesses (Stewart, 2013).

Contribution to Business Practice

Business leaders may benefit from the themes and innovations derived from this study. Business leaders and stakeholders who gain knowledge about natural hazards may have a better understanding of the need to plan for disasters (Kantur & İşeri-Say, 2015; Kellens, Terpstra, & De Maeyer, 2012). Leaders of new businesses may also benefit from the results of this study by understanding the link between business continuity and business survival in the aftermath of a natural disaster. The findings of this study contribute to the body of knowledge in the field by illustrating the successful uses of emergency plans that maintain business continuity and prevent business failure.

Implications for Social Change

The results of this study may affect, or bring about, positive social change. Business leaders may use the findings from this study to gain new insights into what type of planning is necessary to survive a natural disaster. Thus, new business owners could begin to seek successful approaches to model to establish good practices that promote business continuity in disastrous situations. Seasoned small business leaders without business continuity plans, or who are reluctant to revise strategies already in place, could rethink their attitudes toward disaster planning or revise outdated business continuity plans to include preplanning and recovery plans for natural disasters (Lamanna et al., 2012). Other interested parties may be insurance adjusters who specialize in natural disasters. Small business owners that plan for natural disasters may increase socio–environmental awareness, thus reducing the negative effect of climate change and global warming.

A Review of the Professional and Academic Literature

My focus in the literature review for this qualitative multiple case study was to explore how some small business owners in northeastern Florida have avoided permanent business closure in the aftermath of a natural disaster. In this literature review, I supported the interrelationship between the constructs of this study and the research problem. The strategy for the review was a broad, contemporary, focused search of scholarly, peer-reviewed journal articles, books, and electronic media across multiple disciplines.

Organization of the Review

The principal sources of data I used for the review of literature included search engines from Walden University, Jacksonville University, and the University of North Florida libraries. Databases included Business Source Complete, ABI/INFORM ProQuest, SAGE Premier, Google Scholar, Wiley, EBSCOhost, Science Direct, ProQuest, and Elsevier. I used the following search keywords to locate literature for this review: *natural disasters, the theory of planned behavior, vested interest theory, small business, business continuity, preparedness, recovery plans,* and *small businesses in northeastern Florida.* The basis of the literature review of this study was to provide a comprehensive review of themes and topics found in the literature related to avoiding permanent business closure in the aftermath of a natural disaster.

I developed this review of the literature on natural disaster preparedness within small businesses using three topics: (a) critical analysis and synthesis of the conceptual framework, (b) critical analysis and synthesis of literature and themes, and (c) analysis and synthesis of the literature of supplementary themes. The literature review will conclude with an analysis of the synthesis of additional themes related to how leaders of small businesses in northeastern Florida avoided permanent closure in the aftermath of a natural disaster. I included the common and supplemental themes in Table 1.

Table 1

Common and Supplemental Themes

Common themes	Supplemental themes
Small business and the aftermath of natural disasters	Small business and climate change
Small business natural disaster emergency management	Natural disaster types and their effect on small business
Small business closures and Florida natural disasters	Tropical Storm Beryl
	Small business continuity
Small business leaders and natural disaster	Small business financing and insurance
	Small business opportunities and continuing employment
	Small business politics, education, and training

Strategy for Searching the Literature

I identified and evaluated more than 700 articles published over a period of 18 months and included 181 relevant studies in this literature review. The extensive review of articles includes 173 peer-reviewed articles published between 2012 and 2016 and eight published in 2011 or earlier. The peer–reviewed percentage of sources published within 5 years was 87.24%. My review of literature also included the analysis of four books. Appendix A contains the number of literature sources used (see Table A2), and Table A3 includes the sources of the literature over the years.

In this study, 90.62% of the source literature had a publication date between 2012 and 2016 and met the 85% requirement set by the university.

Critical Analysis and Synthesis of the Conceptual Frameworks

The purpose of this qualitative multiple case study was to explore strategies business owners in northeastern Florida have used to avoid permanent business closure in the aftermath of a natural disaster. The population for the study were retail and wholesale small business owners in northeastern Florida. Providing positive social change was a goal of this study. The implications for positive social change from this study may include a better understanding of how natural disasters can affect business continuity. The findings may benefit four distinct groups: new small business entrepreneurs, business owners with a disaster plan that needs updating, small business owners in northeastern Florida, and disaster readiness organizations throughout the state of Florida.

An analysis and synthesis of the literature on TPB and VI theory serve as a means for understanding how small business leaders survive and recover from natural disasters. I will discuss TPB and VI theories using supporting and contrasting views related to the literature. Completing this literature review also involved analyzing and synthesizing other models that supported or contrasted with TPB and VI theory.

Critical analysis and synthesis of the theory of planned behavior (TPB). Small business owners attitudes toward disaster may influence decision making. Thomas and Znaniecki (1918) developed the concept of attitude. Ajzen and Fishbein developed the theory of reasoned action in 1969 and used the theory as a lens to understand how people performed actions based on voluntary intentions (Ajzen, 1985). Ajzen (1985) noted intentions do not always materialize into expected behavior, as there is a missing factor involved with behavioral outcomes. Conversely, Uţă and Popescu (2013) identified attitudes as having several components: cognitive, as related to an individual's perceptions; affective, as the way a person feels about the subject; and conative, based on a specific behavior.

Ajzen extended the theory of reasoned action in 1985 into the TPB by including a control factor (Gagnon, Cassista, Payne-Gagnon, & Martel, 2015; Strang, 2014). Making decisions involves subjective factors, with the result being the behavior performed (Ajzen, 2005). Of the three constructs of the theory, including subjective norms and attitudes, the perception of control has played a significant role in intentional behavior (Perry & Langley, 2013; Sánchez-Medina, Romero-Quintero & Sosa-Cabrera, 2014; Wang & Ritchie, 2012). Intentions to prepare for a disaster elicit a positive feeling of being in control of the future (Gagnon et al., 2015). In a study of small to mid–sized companies, 38% of the intentions to use environmental planning came from the attitude toward the behavior (Sánchez-Medina et al., 2014).

Managers may increase their understanding of climate change through the expansive view of planned behavior (Chen, 2016). Ajzen, Joyce, Sheikh, and Cote (2011) noted that TPB was a predictor of behavior. Knowledge, values, and a high locus of control have produced environmental practices (Williams & Schaefer, 2013). Business owners may develop a better understanding of the negative effects extreme weather by creating disaster plans.

Critical analysis and synthesis of vested interest (VI) theory. The other conceptual framework associated with this study was Crano's (1983) VI theory. Sivacek and Crano (1982) conducted a conceptual study on college students inquiring about their interest in changing the legal age to drink alcohol from 18 to 21 years old. Sivacek and Crano suggested students who were 18 years old had a higher VI in a change to the law. Individuals' perceptions of anticipated personal and meaningful consequences occurring quickly from the result of the behavior (i.e., immediacy) strengthen or weaken their beliefs about their VI levels (Miller et al., 2013).

Self-efficacy refers to a person's belief in his or her ability to generate change or the desired outcome (Crano, 1983; Miller et al., 2013). Adame and Miller (2016) assumed a person is normally aware that natural disasters are dangerous and suggested that increasing a person's disaster awareness would also increase self–efficacy. Self–efficacy empowers individuals with a sense of confidence when preparing for natural disasters (Alipour et al., 2015; Samaddar, Chatterjee, Misra, & Tatano, 2014). Furthermore, skills in natural disaster preparedness may help support positive self–efficacy behaviors (Melnikov, Itzhaki, & Kagan, 2013). Positive, relevant situations have created attitudes coupled with the perceived meaningfulness of the consequences and resulted in a positive stake in the attitude–relevant behavior (De Dominics et al., 2014). Business owners self–efficacy belief of overcoming disasters may be critical in surviving the aftermath.

Existing research supports a link between people's attitudes and behaviors; however, the importance given to people's attitudes can vary emotionally, cognitively, contextually, or culturally (Adame & Miller, 2016; Crano & Prislin, 1995; Miller et al., 2013). In conjunction with the VI theory, known factors that can affect people's level of vesting in attitudes and behaviors include salience, certainty, immediacy, and self–efficacy (Adame & Miller, 2016; De Dominicis et al., 2014). The salience of attitude refers to a person's perceived readiness or accessibility to act upon or interact with his or her committed beliefs (Miller et al., 2013). Miller et al. (2013) developed scales to assess levels of VI related to people's attitudes toward earthquake and tornado preparedness. Business owners may use scales to access stakeholders attitude toward disaster planning.

An individual's perceived certainty of personal consequences resulting from attitude–relevant behavior has shown strong moderation related to VI levels (Adame & Miller, 2016). Residents who reside in the Midwest and Southeast regularly experience hurricanes and tornadoes (Miller et al., 2013). Environmental factors often influence and maintain perceptions of certainty. Business owners that frequently experience damage and destruction from natural disasters may have a better understanding of the importance of planning.

Supporting and contrasting views on theory of planned behavior (TPB). Planned actions by stakeholders have affected disaster prevention effectiveness (Kim, Ham, Yang, & Choi, 2013). For example, in a study of 201 stakeholder respondents, perceived disaster risk reduction, proactive natural disaster planning, and optimistic bias increased during a 12–month non–storm period using pro–environmental education (Trumbo, Meyer, Marlatt, Peek, & Morrissey, 2013). Researchers have supported using TPB as a lens for understanding behavior (Ejeta, Ardalan, & Paton, 2015; Gagnon et al., 2015; Hirano, Kishi, Narupiti, Choocharukul, & Nakatsuji, 2014; Mancha & Yoder, 2015; Su & Ni, 2013; Walker & Redmond, 2014). The most important antecedent of the TPB may be preparedness (Mancha & Yoder, 2015). Business owners perceive environmental dangers differently, and individuals can analyze their responses to natural disasters using TPB (Bullough, Renko, & Myatt, 2014).

Similarly, self–efficacy, which is a component of VI theory, parallels with the TPB control factor, for instance, supplying a person with resources and skill to increase the likelihood of that person carrying out the intended behavior (Ajzen, 1985). Using self–efficacy and other factors to formulate natural disaster strategies can be valuable when combined with TBP as a framework lens (Choi, 2012). Implementing natural disaster strategies depends on managers using positive self–efficacy (Wang & Ritchie, 2012).

Divergent views of planned behavior have indicated a lack of focus on subliminal and irrational thought processes (Strang, 2014; Walker & Redmond, 2014). There are different opinions on the effectiveness of planned behavior. Smith (2012) noted that Perugini and Bagozzi believed their motivation–goal–behavior (MGB) model was more appropriate than the TPB when actions are a means to an end. A divergent view of perceived behavioral control is the belief that all actions are voluntary (Strang, 2014). However, Strang (2014) indicated that control was not a predictor of behavior in disaster planning in some situations because people often have a choice to stay or leave. The perceived behavioral control behavior factor was relevant for individuals with disabilities during Hurricane Sandy because of their physical limitations (Strang, 2014). Conversely, Chien, Yen, and Hoang (2012) noted TPB had limitations in the ability to predict automatic muscle memory actions. Planned behavior may not fully explain the decision to prepare or not prepare for the aftermath of natural disasters.

Supporting and contrasting views on vested interest (VI) theory. Humans who live in regions prone to a higher risk of natural disasters are more likely to develop strong attitudes and views regarding the potential danger with higher degrees of certainty about the outcomes (Crano & Prislin, 1995). In contrast, Oklahoma residents who were used to natural disaster threats were likely to feel indifferent because of the number of false alarms they experienced compared to actual tornadoes, which also indicated their degree of sensitivity to threats was low (Miller et al., 2013). Oklahoma has the highest tornado frequency in the United States (Miller et al., 2013).

A sample of 252 business owners in Afghanistan with the ability to develop a greater belief of self–efficacy embraced strategies to maintain and sustain business during a crisis (Bullough et al., 2014). In contrast, in a study of 2,000 participants, natural disasters had no positive effect on self–efficacy (Monllor & Altay, 2016). Self–efficacy includes a focus on an individual's actions and ability to influence the outcome of a situation (Alipour et al., 2015). In a study of 28 business school professors and 386 organizational behavior students, self–efficacy increased through support from fellow students, employees, and management (Choi, 2012). Proactive natural disaster planning behavior implemented by an administration often results in reduced employee self–efficacy (Smith & O'Sullivan, 2012).

Conceptual models supporting and contrasting with the theory of planned behavior (TPB). Using TPB as a framework, Wang, and Ritchie (2012) revealed how changing cultural norms and empowering stakeholders influenced cultural change and stakeholder empowerment attitudes toward natural disaster planning. To understand the process of changing an organization's behavior, Mancha and Yoder (2015) created a conceptual model called environmental planned behavior theory using 162 participants to change the intentional behavior toward the environment. Mancha and Yoder suggested using pro–environmental policies with a focus on individuals and specific groups within an organization to change their intentions toward preparedness.

Motter and Campbell (2013) contended that chaos theory, developed by Lorenz in 1963, could be a lens to predict natural disasters. Lorenz believed the flap of a butterfly's wing could cause weather patterns to change (Motter & Campbell, 2013). VI theory, created by Crano in 1983, applies to the context of motivated behavior in crisis situations (De Dominicis et al., 2014; Miller et al., 2013). The secondary appraisal process not only initiates immediate coping behaviors but also, given time and cognitive elaboration, leads to perceptions of self-efficacy and motivations to act in the face of threats or opportunities (Miller et al., 2013). When humans determine there is no possibility of a negative outcome from a situation, trying to elicit risk–avoidance behavior can be a challenge; therefore, understanding ways to boost appropriate responses to hazardous environmental events is critical (De Dominicis et al., 2014).

Several theoretical models, including systems and decision theory, include components suitable for developing leadership plans for disaster recovery (Johnson & Hayashi, 2012). Strategic management is an important topic from the perspectives of chaos theory and systems theory in turbulent, chaotic environments (Taneja, Pryor, Humphreys, & Singleton, 2013). Complex systems theory with seemingly the same causes has different effects, so people cannot assume they know the actual outcome implications of some cases (Cox, 2012).

Conceptual models supporting and contrasting with vested interest (VI) theory. Miller et al. (2013) mentioned the person-relative-to–event theory, noting that individual self–reliance and mitigating resources equal to the force of a natural disaster might neutralize the adverse effects of the disaster. Lindell and Perry's protective action decision model could help frame a disaster preparedness plan based on decisions made from taking environmental cues, self–efficacy, and other pertinent information (Miller et al., 2013). Individuals can be ready for disasters, but should only respond if they believe they are capable; otherwise, they should not engage. Adame et al. (2013) extended the parallel process model of fear appeals into an index that measures VI components such as attitudes related to disaster preparedness. VI has not maintained consistency with moderating the attitude element of humans (De Dominicis et al., 2014; Sivacek & Crano, 1982). Individuals must believe they can survive a natural disaster. Other researchers have identified communicative and perceptual issues for business leaders regarding natural disasters, such as lack of self–efficacy and response efficacy among residents in flood-prone areas (Strang, 2014).

Critical Analysis and Synthesis of Literature and Themes

The focus of the literature that I will discuss in this section is lessons from business leaders who survived natural disasters. I will primarily concentrate on studies whose authors developed solutions to small business closures after a natural disaster to create positive attitudes through using the conceptual preparedness framework. Disaster and recovery planning is the first step toward disaster continuity (Epstein & Khan, 2014; Momani & Fadil, 2013; Morrison, Titi Oladunjouye, & Dembry, 2014). Several common themes emerged, including how small businesses in northeastern Florida may survive the aftermath of a natural disaster. I will also review small business emergency management and natural disasters within the literature. Another major literature review revealed a common theme was small business closures and Florida natural disasters. The last major theme I explored was small business leadership and natural disasters.

Small businesses and the aftermath of natural disasters. In a study of 254 small enterprises in Bangladesh, Khan and Sayem (2013) indicated loans provided before a natural disaster increased resilience and survival in the aftermath of the natural disaster. One out of four affected companies may not be able to reopen after a natural disaster (Guster, Lee, & McCann, 2012; Randolph, 2015). Operational information lost during a catastrophe results in almost half of the affected businesses not reopening, and a little more than half will go out of business in less than 2 years (Sasirekha, 2013).

Successful business leaders can view a natural disaster from a broad perspective while separating it into components and patterns (Samuel, Quinn Griffin, White, & Fitzpatrick, 2015). In a study of small businesses struck by a natural disaster, successful strategies included disaster funding, preparedness strategies, and alternate sites for extra inventory (Kunz, Reiner, & Gold, 2014). Alternative locations for supplies or inventory are imperative after a natural disaster if vendor delays occur or if business leaders must find new suppliers, which could take weeks (Kunz et al., 2014).

Few researchers have focused on small businesses after a natural disaster (Marshall, Niehm, Sydnor, & Schrank, 2015). Many natural disasters have affected companies in heavily populated areas because of the vast number of buildings and human lives affected, which results in paralyzing damage to the businesses (Xiao & Nilawar, 2013). Business recovery plans should involve key stakeholders within local districts (Johnson & Hayashi, 2012). The best natural disaster recovery plan may be one designed for a particular business (Berke, Cooper, Aminto, Grabich, & Horney, 2014).

Johnson and Hayashi (2012) also noted that taking inventory of economic damage is one of the first actions needed after a natural disaster. The primary aim of recovery plans is to reestablish operations in the shortest amount of time, with minimal damage (Prazeres & Lopes, 2013). Businesses with multiple sources of assistance (e.g., private and public donors) recover from natural disasters faster (Asgary et al., 2012).

Small business leaders may have a limited ability to plan for every threat that happens in the recovery phase (Morrison et al., 2014). Leaders may maintain operations after a catastrophe through network collaboration established with another business leader before a disastrous event occurs (Howat et al., 2012; Priscoli & Stakhiv, 2015). Recovery factors that lead to rapid recovery are employees, knowledge, and skill of management, stable monetary position, patron support, and resource mitigation efforts (Wai & Wongsurawat, 2013).

After the 2010 floods in Pakistan, government leaders enacted stronger building codes (Asgary et al., 2012). Most Pakistani small businesses reopened within 6 months after the natural disaster (Asgary et al., 2012). Survival depended on having immediate access to finances (Asgary et al., 2012). In a survey of leaders from 376 businesses after the Canterbury earthquake in New Zealand, respondents indicated that sound buildings, employee health, and customer retention played a major role in never losing business continuity throughout the disaster (Whitman et al., 2014).

Firms that have an annex site set up away from the disaster–stricken area can maintain continuity and operations such as human resources, information technology, and other vital operations (Atkinson & Sapat, 2014; Lamanna et al., 2012; Xiao & Drucker, 2013). In contrast, in a study of businesses struck by flooding in Thailand, 80% of the businesses decided not to relocate but instead decided to scale down their business in preparation for future floods (Hayakawa, Matsuura & Okubo, 2015). Also, business leaders who relocate their businesses should consider the time it takes to reestablish a business and build relationships with customers (Pérez-Nordtvedt, O'Brien, & Rasheed, 2013).

Small business emergency management and natural disasters. The main stages involved in disaster management are before, during, and immediately following a catastrophe (Prochazkova, 2013; Randolph, 2015). In 2011, FEMA leaders launched the Plan, Prepare, and Mitigate campaign to ensure proper actions before, during, and after a disaster (Randolph, 2015). Employers received encouragement from FEMA staff to protect employees and properties from future disasters by developing or reviewing emergency response and business continuity plans. The main goal of emergency preparedness plans is to protect employees and business owners (Randolph, 2015).

The literature on disaster management dates to the 1980s. The first use of the term appeared in 1979 by FEMA in Canada (Hémond & Benoît, 2012; Sahebjamnia et al., 2015). The extent and severity of natural disasters continue to limit the effectiveness of human–made attempts to curb their effects (Prochazkova, 2013). Since the mid–1970s, hurricanes have been the deadliest natural disasters and have been responsible for nearly 750,000 casualties (Prochazkova, 2013). Floods and earthquakes ranked second and third most dangerous, respectively, with approximately 200,000 deaths each (Prochazkova, 2013). By 2011, substantial efforts to manage disaster situations more effectively intensified, as the need for emergency preparedness planning was evident due to recent natural disasters occurring around the world (Randolph, 2015).

Education and training. More emphasis on educating the leaders of privately owned small businesses is necessary to instigate disaster planning behavior changes (Saarinen, Hambira, Atlhopheng, & Manwa, 2012; Trumbo et al., 2013). Disaster education may ensure resource support from donors after a disaster (Walker & Redmond, 2014). Disaster education involves incorporating documented experiences and training programs (Altay et al., 2013).

Scenario anticipation through training and development are critical for decreasing the severity of crises (Hernantes, Rich, Laugé, Labaka, & Sarriegi, 2013). Business leaders should conduct periodic training and mock drills to reinforce employees' behavior during disasters (Randolph, 2015). Training for disasters should include formal procedures; for example, during normal business operations, employees should remain relaxed during the implementation of the crisis plan (Randolph, 2015; Van der Vegt, Essens, Wahlström, & George, 2015).

In preparing for natural disasters, employee training, active participation, and competencies can empower organizational leaders by identifying individual employee needs (Eiser et al., 2012). Training on natural disasters should occur in collaboration with local governmental agencies (Izumi & Shaw, 2014). Additionally, small business preparedness strategies should include disaster drills for employees (Hoong & Marthandan, 2014). Some employees believe disaster training increases the overtime pay of the training instructor, which has resulted in negative attitudes toward catastrophe planning training (Wang & Ritchie, 2012).

Planning. Some business disaster plans include national response elements related to preparedness (Randeree, Mahal, & Narwani, 2012) and disaster training and drill exercises (Mannakkara & Wilkinson, 2014). Also, included as a preparedness response element are an education (Daramola, Oni, Ogundele, & Adesanya, 2016), business contacts (utilities, suppliers, and employees), regular inventories, and stockpiling equipment and supplies. Other elements included alternative sites for businesses, making prearrangements with vendors, and contacting backup vendors to provide basic needs or necessary equipment (Medina, 2016). Other necessary elements include duplicate records of building plans, insurance policies, supplier lists, bank account records and tax records (3 years for insurance purposes), and a list of law enforcement contacts (Medina, 2016).

Promoting the advantages of disaster prevention while planning may change the mind–set of stakeholders who do not believe disaster plans prevent business closure (Kunreuther & Weber, 2014). Furthermore, business leaders are not attending to disaster preparedness to the degree necessary to prevent business closure (Morrison et al., 2014).

Small business leaders without disaster plans assume they have the ability to plan for a disaster even though they did not have a disaster plan (Herbane, 2013).

More organizational leaders are employing risk-based strategies by building partnerships based on business continuity and disaster recovery organizations (Epstein & Khan, 2014). Baba, Watanabe, Nagaishi and Matsumoto (2014) speculated that socioeconomic job losses because of catastrophic hazards increased the need for private–public partnership disaster mitigation plans. Leaders of small businesses can align themselves with risk-reducing means and implement company–wide natural disaster strategies (Baba et al., 2014). Private–public partnerships have led to cost reductions and increased trust among members of the business community (Vinayagamoorthy, 2014).

Positive disaster intentions can be enhanced using crafted plans that signify business leaders are demonstrating the behavior needed for a future crisis (Lindström, 2012). Key natural disaster preparation strategies related to survival include social values and family togetherness (Asgary et al., 2012). Preparing for disasters requires every member of an organization to prepare together with any outside resources available (Sahebjamnia et al., 2015). Focused and increased security is important to consider when planning for disasters (Izumi & Shaw, 2014). Guiding questions related to natural disaster prevention and recovery may include a focus on the participants' experiences before, during, and after major hurricanes (Howat et al., 2012).

In 2011, less than half of business owners engaged in disaster preparedness (Asgary et al., 2012). Factors to consider before a crisis include identifying the probability of natural disasters happening in the area (Ikse & Lengfellner, 2015).

Business leaders should know their company's ability to maintain operations following a disaster (Ikse & Lengfellner, 2015).

Collaborating with public and private leaders is essential to forming a disaster plan. Preventing business failure following catastrophes involves avoiding areas known for hazards and retrofitting structures based on local codes (Izumi & Shaw, 2014; Xiao & Nilawar, 2013). Collaborating with officials and avoiding disaster zones may benefit small business leaders. Leaders of nonprofits and public companies prepare more for natural disasters (Chikoto, Sadiq, & Fordyce, 2013).

After a natural disaster, business leaders need to collaborate with their disaster network with a sense of urgency (Sawalha, Jraisat, & Al-Qudah, 2013). A checklist can increase coordination and collaboration with all stakeholders during a natural disaster (Steelman & McCaffrey, 2013). Preparedness plans reduce chaos. In a qualitative study after Hurricane Katrina, Chamlee-Wright and Storr (2014) interviewed business leaders who created relationships and designated locations at the workplace where friendship networks developed before disasters. The network relationships helped prevent business closure in the aftermath of the disaster (Chamlee-Wright & Storr, 2014).

In a qualitative study conducted by Gin, Kranke, Saia, and Dobalian (2016), participants discovered how network partnerships, education, and disaster planning prevented business closure. Another study included data that indicated external agencies had limitations regarding their ability to assist businesses during a disaster (Gin et al., 2016). Business leaders need to choose only the essential functions needed to maintain business continuity during and after a disaster (Gin et al., 2016). Consequently, business leaders should form relationships of trust with other businesses in the community (Chamlee-Wright & Storr, 2014; Dufty, 2012).

Developing a business networking space near or in a small business allows for collaboration and relationship building (Chamlee-Wright & Storr, 2014). Private–public partnerships create insurance against business closures in the aftermath of natural disasters (Galeotti, Gürtler, & Winkelvos, 2012). Using a cognitive strategy related to social norms that emphasize the importance of short– and long–term disaster planning may alter managers' attitudes on implementation (Wang & Ritchie, 2012).

Natural disaster effects on small business closures in Florida. Florida business owners suffered complete devastation from hurricanes in 1926 and 1928 (Boustan et al., 2012). Nearly 60% of all Category 4 or higher hurricanes hit Florida and Texas (Blake et al., 2007). In May 1863, an unprecedented hurricane hit northwest Florida, making it the only recorded strike outside the normal hurricane season in U.S. history (Chenoweth & Mock, 2013). The 1928 Okeechobee Hurricane was a Category 4 hurricane that killed an estimated 1,836 people (Boustan et al., 2012; Marchigiani et al., 2013). In 1935, a Category 5 hurricane in Florida devastated the region, and over the next several decades, the frequency of storms increased during record-setting hurricane seasons (Blake et al., 2007; Marchigiani et al., 2013).

The hurricane seasons in 2004 and 2005 included 28 tropical storms and 15 hurricanes. Although the casualties from Hurricanes Ivan and Frances in 2004 were relatively small, the cost to reestablish the communities in Florida and Alabama was almost $30 billion (Blake et al., 2007). At least 40% of U.S. hurricanes hit Florida (Blake et al., 2007). The economic impact in the eastern Atlantic and Florida from Hurricane Wilma in 2005 was an estimated $28.9 million (Chatterjee & Mozumder, 2015). Wilma disrupted over 3.2 million out of 4 million Florida Power & Light electrical company subscribers (Chatterjee & Mozumder, 2015). Hurricanes may continue to compromise the safety and well–being of millions of people unless appropriate actions minimize their adverse effects.

Some business leaders have included the possibility of business closure, as well as staffing factors and the loss of vital services in their disaster plans (Lamanna et al., 2012). However, mitigating future catastrophes may prevent business closure (Smith & Sutter, 2013). One out of four companies will not reopen after a flood, tornado, earthquake, or hurricane (Randolph, 2015).

Small Business Natural Disaster Leadership

Successful strategies for preparing for and recovering from natural disasters can come from multiple stakeholders (e.g., employees, managers, and business leaders), rather than from one silo approach (Baba et al., 2014; Eiser et al., 2012; Galeotti et al., 2012). There remains a great divide among business leaders related to the perceived causes of natural disasters (Miller et al., 2013). However, successful implementation of readiness strategies may prevent small businesses from failing and increase their chances of surviving a natural disaster (Sawalha, 2014). This section includes a discussion on business owners and managers' perceptions of disaster preparedness.

Small business owners. Thirty–six percent of business leaders studied by Miller et al. (2013) thought the impact of climate change on their business was high, and 79%

thought climate change was a legitimate threat. Business leaders' perceptions vary regarding how much preparation is necessary for natural disasters (Morrison et al., 2014). In a study of 111 managers and owners, 64% thought the impact of climate change on their individual businesses was low, and 21% did not believe in climate change (Walker & Redmond, 2014). Herbane (2013) noted that experience and the type of disaster factored into managers' decisions on whether they developed disaster plans.

In the 1800s, flooding was the major disaster problem for entrepreneurs (Priscoli & Stakhiv, 2015). Greed was a contributing factor in the decision to develop land in hazardous areas in the early 1900s, as business leaders constructed and reconstructed after natural disasters in known disaster–zoned areas (Pidot, 2013). In the 1950s and 1960s, business owners decided on the need for alternate storage locations to prevent the loss of electronic files after a natural disaster (Randeree et al., 2012).

A link may exist between the amount of time a business owner resides in a community and a lower sensitivity to emergency hazard awareness (Trumbo et al., 2013). Business owners have historically built in some coastal areas where hurricanes have caused major destruction (Herbane, 2010). After Hurricane Katrina, 62% of business owners stated the biggest problem was a lack of customers and a loss of sales (Schrank et al., 2013).

Business owners are more likely than managers are to make adaptive disaster mitigation improvements to their buildings (Wedawatta, Ingirige, & Proverbs, 2013). Business owners with higher education have a more positive effect on their company (Khan & Sayem, 2013). Acquiring disaster mitigation tools also helps mitigate the effect of natural disasters, but the acquisition had no positive effect on the negative employee attitudes toward company disaster prevention (Khan & Sayem, 2013).

In the past, business owners developed liability plans related to their specific small business in anticipation of a disaster (Atkinson & Sapat, 2014). Ninety-four percent of small proprietors in one study noted they benefited more from grants than from coverage premiums (De Mel et al., 2012). Business owners should look for well–priced catastrophic insurance premiums that reduce monetary damages by providing higher benefit payments (Kaushalya, Karunasena, & Amarathunga, 2014; Kunreuther, Michel-Kerjan, & Pauly, 2013).

Small business managers. Managerial attitudes changed after the terrorist attacks on September 11, 2001, the strategic intent changed to business continuity management (Herbane, 2010). Many managers perceive disaster planning as a secondary operation (Herbane, 2010; Morrison, 2014; Smith & O'Sullivan, 2012). In a quantitative study on climate change, managers' beliefs in climate change existence played a major role in developing a natural disaster plan (Chen, 2016). Some managers' beliefs about climate change are contrary to analytical forecasts (Kunreuther & Weber, 2014).

Managers whose attitudes reflect a choice not to embrace the adverse effect of catastrophes may jeopardize the company's ability to withstand a disaster (Herbane, 2010). Personal attitudes of managers may have a direct effect on disaster preparedness (Wibbenmeyer, Hand, Calkin, Venn, & Thompson 2013). Further study of the relationship between industry characteristics and manager attitudes toward disaster planning may contribute to the body of literature (Herbane, 2013).

Managers of small enterprises noted that motivation was the most important factor in being proactive (Williams & Schaefer, 2013). Managers' negative beliefs reduce other employees' willingness to plan for natural disasters (Chen, 2016). Management flexibility during a catastrophe leads to better communication through all phases of the disaster (Steelman & McCaffrey, 2013).

Analysis and Synthesis of Literature of Supplementary Themes

The following subsections will include discussions of several supplemental themes. The first will be small businesses and climate change, and the next theme will be the negative effect of natural disasters on small businesses. The third supplemental theme will be Tropical Storm Beryl, followed by small business continuity, small business financing and insurance, small business opportunities, and continuing employment.

Small businesses and climate change. Fourier first described climate change as the greenhouse effect in 1824, but perspectives shifted 70 years later in 1896 to carbon emissions (Smith & Bond, 2014; Vlassopoulos, 2012). High global mean greenhouse gas concentrations have human influences (Taylor, Bruine de Bruin, & Dessai, 2014). Taylor et al. (2014) noted the greenhouse gas effect resulted from higher earth surface temperatures. The global external atmosphere increased between 1900 and 1940, according to the *Fifth Assessment Report of the Intergovernmental Panel on Climate* (Bayer, Pugh, Krause, & Arneth, 2015; Taylor et al., 2014). Climate changes caused by human–related factors increased from 1951 through 2010 (Taylor et al., 2014).

A global warming trend occurred in the mid–1960s and 1970s (Friedland & Hare, 2007). The trend of extreme temperature increases is the result of natural changes in the atmosphere that do not relate to human causes (Dulière, Zhang, & Salathé, 2013; Mika, 2013). Atmospheric aerosols such as sulfur and carbon may affect the climate's heating and cooling process (Tiwari et al., 2016). For example, aerosols used from the 1950s to the 1970s had a cooling effect on the Earth's temperature (Smith & Bond, 2014). Eliminating sulfur from the atmosphere also increased the Earth's surface temperature (Dulière et al., 2013). The aerosol cooling effect of sulfur does not compare to the warming created by carbon emissions because the carbon remains in the atmosphere, which creates the greenhouse effect (Smith & Bond, 2014).

In a study of 33 small snowmaking businesses, climate adaptation was relative based on the business location (Hopkins, 2014). Perceptions influence decision making by business leaders. The inconsistency of natural disasters may delay intentions on climate change adaptation (Welle, 2012). Planning through learning and capability are important factors in adjusting to climate change (Lei & Wang, 2014; Matzenberger et al., 2015).

Various natural disasters and political effects on small business. Extreme geological events consist of tsunamis, landslides, avalanches, volcanic eruptions, blizzards, heat waves, and sinkholes (Pidot, 2013). In the United States, the dust bowl of the 1930s was one of the worst drought-related natural disasters in history (Boustan et al., 2012; Kousky, 2014). Similarly, today business leaders in San Francisco did not learn from the earthquakes that occurred in 1868 and 1906 (Dyl, 2009). Experts had predicted a considerable amount of destruction would result from earthquakes like the 1989 San Francisco Loma Prieta earthquake because of forecasted probabilities. Scientists knew the Valencia Street Hotel sat on gravel–filled lakebed before its implosion during the 1906 earthquake (Dyl, 2009). After the Northridge earthquake in 1994, business leaders started to focus more on disaster preparedness to prevent business closures (Levy et al., 2016).

Small businesses around the world experience significant losses each year, including failure as a direct result of natural disasters (Monllor & Altay, 2016). Donors' resources can help to rebuild to prevent business closures (Khan & Sayem, 2013). Another strategy small business leaders have used to maintain business continuity is providing refuge for employees made homeless by a disaster in exchange for free labor to repair structurally damaged businesses (Chamlee–Wright & Storr, 2014). Natural disasters destroy commerce and jeopardize society (Marchigiani et al., 2013).

Pro–environmental norms have positively shaped communication behaviors (Teng, Wu, & Liu, 2015). For example, Baba et al. (2014) explained how disaster communication formulation alerts all stakeholders of a disaster plan. Business destruction from floods and hurricanes affects not only businesses but also the socioeconomics lives of the employees and their families (Morrison et al., 2014).

Politics. Politics affects the outcomes of natural disasters. Government leaders created a national policy for disasters in the early 19th century. In 1884, disaster victims did not receive aid following a tornado in North Carolina because government leaders did not consider it a national or geographically widespread event (Davies, 2014). Business leaders needed additional sources for recovery relief. The Federal Disaster Act of 1950 created the presidential declaration of catastrophe. The passage of this statute largely confined Red Cross workers to assisting persons without property and property owners whom federal officials regard as poor credit risks, which limited the government to providing support mostly to disaster victims who were more likely able to help themselves (Goshay, Dacy, & Kunreuther, 1970).

Initial efforts by the U.S. federal government to address flooding disasters were somewhat futile. Unsuccessful attempts by the legislature to pass a water hazard law lasted from 1959 to 1967 (Collier & Lakoff, 2014; Myers, 1975). The Later legislation attempts to provide assistance for water-related damages were unsuccessful due to large–scale uninsured flood claims. Furthermore, individuals and communities who did not participate were not eligible to receive disaster relief or reimbursements for losses due to floods (Kunreuther et al., 2013).

Disaster mitigation should include noninfrastructure and infrastructure efforts that reduce businesses' exposure to catastrophes (Palliyaguru, Amaratunga, & Baldry, 2014). The scope and rigor of natural disasters have continued to define the effectiveness or lack of effectiveness of human–created structures designed to mitigate natural disasters (Prochazkova, 2013). De Souza, Yukio, and Dollery (2015) contended that infrastructure is the focus of any disaster recovery planning.

Government leaders can assist with business continuity by upgrading public community systems (Clarke & Grenham, 2013). Proactive management and business continuity may bring companies closer to federal regulation compliance (Baba et al., 2014). Conversely, government stakeholders may expect businesses to have a backup plan for continued services after a natural disaster (Epstein & Khan, 2014; Momani & Fadil, 2013; Morrison et al., 2014).

Flooding. Floods usually occur when dry pieces of land submerge in water from a weather event (Blöschl et al., 2015). There are different types of floods (e.g., coastal floods and small or large river floods) caused by various factors such as tsunamis, continuous rainfall, melting snow, or strong winds and high tides combined (Bloschl et al., 2015). In high–elevation areas, flash floods produce landslides and debris flows (Blöschl et al., 2015). Human alterations or manufactured changes to natural structures may contribute to flooding (Wharton, 2012).

Between 1963 and 2012, storm surges and accompanying flooding caused the most death and destruction from natural disasters in the United States (Rappaport, 2014). The Rapid City Flood of 1972 occurred during the night in South Dakota and resulted in 238 deaths and $160 million in damages (Morris, 2014). The Big Thompson Canyon Flood of 1976 in Colorado left 144 people dead and caused more than $3.5 million in property damage after only one day of flooding (Rasmussen & Houze, 2012). Flatland areas may have a higher chance of flooding. Hurricane Camille in 1969 contributed to hundreds of deaths and caused billions of dollars in physical damage (Priscoli & Stakhiv, 2015; Rappaport, 2014).

The disaster analysis from Hurricane Sandy revealed a need for collaboration between public and private leaders in hopes of alleviating the hazards of increasing flood levels (Rosenzweig & Solecki, 2014). Changing the disaster–planning attitude and intentions of small business leaders may develop business continuity through flood–

planning protection (Wang & Ritchie, 2012). Legislators in Mississippi created a new regulation on how to control flooding in 1927 (Boustan et al., 2012). During a time when the federal budget was $3 billion, the physical damages of $1 billion caused by the Great Flood were crippling (O'Daniel, 2013). The effects of the Great Flood led to flood control legislation that authorized the construction of extensive levee systems built in 1928 (O'Daniel, 2013). After the major flooding of the Ohio and Mississippi Rivers, leaders established water–storing basins in 1937 (Boustan et al., 2012; Collier & Lakoff, 2014). However, the program ended prematurely in 1958 under President Truman from a lack of funding (Myers, 1975).

Hurricanes. After Hurricanes Irene and Sandy, political and social change efforts increased toward saving the environment (Howe, Boudet, Leiserowitz, & Maibach, 2014). Leaders of local and federal governments designed study guides that identified business risks, pinpointed relevant factors within firms, and implemented natural disaster recovery systems (Lyles, Berke, & Smith, 2013). As rising financial costs associated with disasters continue, politicians may see the benefits of disaster risk–reduction planning (Shreve & Kelman, 2014). Business leaders who follow governmental guidelines through planning may improve their infrastructure by preventing or mitigating the effects of natural hazards such as hurricanes.

Hurricanes are a destructive force with varying wind speed and intensity. A hurricane refers to the rapid internal circulation of air masses around an open center, accompanied by adverse weather (Marchigiani et al., 2013). Meteorologists use the Saffir-Simpson Hurricane Wind Scale to measure and classify the intensity of tropical cyclones (Logan & Xu, 2015). Mild hurricanes measured in wind speeds of 74–95 mph are Category 1, and Category 2 hurricanes generate wind speeds between 96 and 100 mph (Blake et al., 2007; NOAA, 2016). Category 3 hurricanes are a major event (111–130 mph), Category 4 hurricanes have winds from 131 to 154 mph, and Category 5 hurricanes have wind speeds higher than 155 mph (Blake et al., 2007; NOAA, 2016).

From 1950 to 1951, North America had a record–setting 13 cyclones (Blake et al., 2007). Hurricane Camille in 1969 was partially responsible for the creation of the Disaster Relief Act of 1970 (Morris, 2014). Hurricane Hugo landed in South Carolina in 1989 and caused $9 billion in damages (Knowles & Kunreuther, 2014). Hurricane Frederic in Alabama and Mississippi in 1979 and Hurricane Andrew in 1992 led to rebuilding costs of $6 billion and $45 billion, respectively (Knowles & Kunreuther, 2014). The southeastern United States, especially coastal areas, has the greatest risk of hurricanes (Husby, de Groot, Hofkes, & Dröes, 2014).

Intense hurricanes can lead to storm surges and flooding, which in turn can lead to unemployment, homelessness, dislocation, migration, and chaos in declared disaster areas (Bowen & Friel, 2012). Destruction because of extreme weather is a rare occurrence, and Trumbo et al. (2013) indicated most businesses survive catastrophes. Older coastal home business residents are optimistic about withstanding a hurricane, whereas newer coastal home business residents listen to the news media and evacuation warnings more frequently (Trumbo et al., 2013). Participants in a study performed immediately after Hurricanes Rita and Katrina had less awareness in a second study presented 2 years later when asked about future storm potential destruction (Trumbo et al., 2013).

The United States has experienced an increasing trend toward costly catastrophic effects caused by hurricanes (Marchigiani et al., 2013). In 2001, Hurricane Allison claimed the lives of 410 people and caused $10 billion in damages (Marchigiani et al., 2013). Hurricane Katrina was the costliest natural disaster in U.S. history (Marchigiani et al., 2013). Hurricane Katrina caused more than 1,200 deaths and over $100 billion in physical damages (Baker, 2014). Hurricanes between 2000 and 2010 were the deadliest in U.S. history (Houston, Pfefferbaum, & Rosenholtz, 2012).

Tornadoes. Tornadoes are masses of turbulent air that extend from the clouds to the ground moving at an accelerated speed (Lopes & Machado, 2015). Tornadoes vary in shape and size, but typically appear as a funnel. Unlike hurricanes, meteorologists classify tornadoes based on their intensity and damaging effects. Between 1875 and 2003, tornado outbreaks accounted for 80% of all natural disaster fatalities; meteorologists recorded more than 58,000 tornadoes in the United States from 1950 to 2013 (Fuhrmann et al., 2014; Lopes & Machado, 2015). The southeastern United States experiences 25 to 35% more tornadoes than the national average (Howe et al., 2014).

The Fujita (F) Scale measured the physical magnitude or strength of tornadoes in the early 1970s, and the national oceanic, atmospheric administration adopted the modification in the United States in February 2007 (Fuhrmann et al., 2014). The Enhanced Fujita (EF) Scale assesses the damage of storms based on a broader selection of buildings and a focus on the estimated maximum speed of the wind (Fuhrmann et al., 2014). The EF Scale captured better damage information related to tornadoes from a wider variety of structures based on the estimated maximum speed of the tornado

(Boustan et al., 2012; Fuhrmann et al., 2014). The intensity of tornadoes varies due to potential damage indicators, such as structures.

Fewer damage indicators are present in less populated (e.g., rural) areas. Weak tornadoes (F/EF0 and F/EF1) occur in small areas in a short period (e.g., a few hours; Fuhrmann et al., 2014). Major tornadoes can involve several strong tornadoes that occur over several states for one or more days (F/EF2 or F/EF3), such as the Super Outbreak of April 1974 and the Widespread Outbreak in November 1992 (Fuhrmann et al., 2014). Violent tornadoes can last for consecutive days (F/EF4 or F/EF5; Fuhrmann et al., 2014).

The Midwest, also known as Tornado Alley, has historically been the most dangerous location for tornadoes because of its temperature changes and weather patterns (Miller et al., 2013). The increase in storms reported may be due to reporting weak tornadoes (Furhmann et al., 2014). Hurricane accuracy has become more consistent over time due to advancements in detection methods and satellite functionalities.

Tropical Storm Beryl

The case in this study is Tropical Storm Beryl (2012). In May 2012, Beryl developed in the Gulf of Mexico and was the strongest pre–seasoned storm in the history of the United States (NOAA, 2016; Zou et al., 2013). By May 27, the tropical storm had gained strength and reached wind speeds of 63 mph before hitting Jacksonville, Florida on May 28. In addition to producing high winds, rain, and thunderstorms, Beryl produced four major tornadoes across the southeastern United States including two tornados in Florida (Zou et al., 2013).

The physical damage included debris, power outages, structural damage to homes and businesses. Beryl's intensity fluctuated and eventually reduced to a tropical depression and tropical wave. Beryl reached conditions associated with a Category 1 hurricane on May 28 (NOAA, 2016; Zou et al., 2013). Tropical Storm Beryl caused death, and 60 homes were damaged, including three mobile trailer homes across the southeastern part of the United States (Stewart, 2013). In the next subsection, I will discuss how financing and insurance may prevent small business closure in the aftermath of a natural disaster.

Small Business Financing and Insurance

The financial cost of business recovery increases the possibility of business closure (Levy et al., 2016). Business leaders need to invest in flood insurance and support government programs that improve business continuity (Asgary et al., 2012). Flood protection sponsored by governmental agencies may prevent permanent business closure by reducing the cost for small businesses (Asgary et al., 2012). Legislative assistance may reduce a firm's susceptibility to natural disasters by proactively helping neutralize financial liability in the local small business population through partnerships between local government and businesses (Atkinson & Sapat, 2014; Farazmand, 2014).

Finance. Business survival depends on a company's financial status and the preparedness measures in place before a disruption occurs (Wai & Wongsurawat, 2013). Access to cash after a natural disaster is a major factor that can determine small business recovery (De Mel, McKenzie, & Woodruff, 2012; Lamanna et al., 2012). Small businesses need many resources in the aftermath of a natural disaster, constraints placed by the government limit the amount companies can receive from public institutions (Linnerooth-Bayer & Hochrainer-Stigler, 2015).

Some business risks during a natural disaster may include potential financial losses or breakdowns in infrastructure, resources, or logistics (Losada, Scaparra, & O'Hanley, 2012; Prazeres & Lopes, 2013; Sahebjamnia et al., 2015; Sasirekha, 2013). Financial strategies for risk reduction may include retraining, reducing, insuring, or transferring the risk (Hamdan, 2015). Consequently, supply chain costs may accumulate during temporary business closures and cause cash flow problems (Herbane, 2013). Developing simulated strategies with a focus on acute and extended natural disasters may reduce the impact of business interruption especially if the simulated disasters have the characteristics of forecasted disasters for a local area (Kusumasari & Alam, 2012).

Tax–exempt private activity bonds are a resource that assists in recovery after a natural disaster (Gotham, 2013). Donors' development projects that engage a community can restore assets and livelihoods (McCarthy, 2014). Also, Dar, Buckley, Rokadiya, Huda and Abrahams (2014) indicated surviving a natural disaster included combining finance, insurance, and good credit. Remarkably, partnerships with governmental public works departments and private businesses provided continuity and strengthen communities (Gotham, 2013).

Insurance. When first implemented, federally subsidized disaster insurance was available to small businesses, churches, and residential structures. Leaders of private firms who could not afford insurance received protection in 1968 (Kunreuther et al., 2013). Risk transfer from hazards includes insurance, personal savings, debt leveraging, donor foundations, and legislative and other resource types (Linnerooth-Bayer et al., 2015). The preferred customers of insurance companies are business owners who operate their business in low–risk flood, hurricane, tornado, or other types of disaster areas (Kaushalya et al., 2014).

Appraisers play an integral role in calculating the components of a casualty loss deduction (Smith & Lougee, 2014). Education or advice from an insurance expert may mean the difference in receiving premiums for repairs after a catastrophe (Smith & Lougee, 2014). Among the most important factors aiding recovery are insurance and business continuity (Asgary et al., 2012).

Small Business Continuity

In the late 1980s, the focus of continuity was on managing unknown environmental opportunities (Sánchez-Medina et al., 2014; Sarmiento et al., 2015). Business continuity plans contain (a) risk analysis, (b) evaluation of infrastructure, (c) business resources, (d) scenarios, and (e) impact analysis (Baba et al., 2014; Randeree et al., 2012; Torabi, Rezaei Soufi, & Sahebjamnia, 2014). Small businesses' success may depend on business leaders' perceptions of disaster planning and the possible adverse effect these perceptions have on business continuity.

Business managers at IBM created continuity related to business in the last half of the 20th century (Herbane, 2010). Guidance is the primary objective of a business continuity plan (Prazeres & Lopes, 2013), yet 56% of leaders' lack continuity plans (Sarmiento et al., 2015). Leaders use a continuity plan to assess the potential business interruption effects of a disaster by gathering knowledge of an adverse situation until business operations commence (Lindström, 2012). Organizations with business continuity recovery plans are more resilient than other organizations (Sahebjamnia et al., 2015). Leaders who apply business continuity management can develop and manage their resources and actions in response to a natural disaster (Herbane, 2013). Business continuity planning is a model for catastrophe hazard management (Baba et al., 2013).

Company–specific risk planning and local natural disaster research are suitable business continuity plans (Baba et al., 2014; Torabi et al., 2014). Additionally, a logistical business continuity plan may provide business leaders with a tentative natural disaster plan that may improve flood immunity (Ojha, Gianiodis, & Manuj, 2013). Efforts to establish continuity strategies based on the changing climate of specific regions may better equip businesses to prepare for future disasters (Baba et al., 2014). Local climate knowledge coupled with skills in disaster mitigation are essential components of emergency planning.

Business Opportunities and Continuing Employment

Business leaders who enhance their continuity can foster the local economy and employment (Baba et al., 2014). Small business opportunities were a major concern during the Fourth International Conference on Building Resilience (Baba et al., 2014). Employees with high self–efficacy that are satisfied with their work ethic may decide to leave their employment after a natural disaster (Baruch, Wordsworth, Mills & Wright, 2015). The manager should do everything they can in the aftermath of a natural disaster in providing for the needs of their employees (Baruch et al., 2015).

Opportunities. There are always chances to improve business processes preceding a natural disaster (Lamanna et al., 2012; Monllor & Altay, 2016). For example, shifting from subsidy–driven to demand–driven business strategies creates small business opportunities after a natural disaster (Izumi & Shaw, 2014). In a study on economic employment data after a catastrophe, Kousky (2014) noted that the construction sector was the most profitable industry after a hurricane, in both the short and the long term. Natural disasters create many opportunities for individuals and groups by improving gender equality for starting businesses (Asgary et al., 2012). Findings from a quantitative study on business opportunities after Hurricane Katrina indicated areas next to the disaster area might realize an increase in demand (Xiao & Nilawar, 2013). Weather–related adaptation involves evaluating and profiting from opportunities while minimizing physical hazards (Hopkins, 2014).

Job creation after a disaster may stimulate economic growth. The construction sector may benefit after a catastrophe because of the need to rebuild (Kousky, 2014). However, long–term construction jobs may slow down after a natural disaster (Kousky, 2014). Economic opportunities were higher in one disaster–stricken area than before the disaster occurred (Monllor & Altay, 2016). Job losses after a catastrophe have not lasted for an extended period (Zissimopoulos & Karoly, 2010).

Other opportunities for small businesses may involve providing drinking water, nutrition, drugs, and building resources during the early stages after a natural disaster; business leaders may put these resources into a disaster risk reduction plan (Izumi & Shaw, 2014). Business opportunities may exist in building materials and related fields

(Penning–Rowsell & Pardoe, 2012). Self–efficacy after a natural disaster may create business opportunities (Monllor & Altay, 2016) and may play a role in capturing market share (C. H. Miller et al., 2013). When exposed to a business opportunity after a natural disaster, self–efficacy strengthens the intention to perform an action successfully (Miller et al., 2013). Self–efficacy coupled with resilience plays a significant role in pursuing business opportunities after a natural disaster (Bullough et al., 2014).

Continuing employment. Xaio and Feser (2013) revealed that economic diversity stimulated employment after the 1993 Midwestern flood. Also, Xaio and Drucker (2013) observed, there was a gap in the literature on the effect diversity plays in community resilience to natural disasters. The traditional labor market changed in response to the impact and recovery activity following Hurricane Bret in 1999 (Ewing, Kruse, & Thompson, 2005). Employment improved after the hurricane, and several economic indicators were constant because of the influx of people migrating into the area for cleanup and construction jobs (Ewing et al., 2005). Conversely, the employment rate from natural disasters was lower 5 or 10 years after the catastrophe (Kousky, 2014).

Jobs in counties affected by floods fell behind jobs in non–flooded counties, but counties affected by flooding had benefited more within 5 years, possibly from the additional aid and other resources infused into the counties after the flood (Xiao & Drucker, 2013). A large market size may reduce vulnerability to failure (Marshall et al., 2015). Arguably, Goshay et al. (1970) indicated long–term disaster recovery referred to achieving a desirable rate of capital re–accumulation. Low unemployment after a natural disaster may occur because of people coming to the area for removal of debris employment, rebuilding, and restoration work (Xiao & Drucker, 2013). Positive effects of a catastrophe include recovery and jobs. Also, the financial sector along with the manufacturing sector showed the most resilience to natural disasters (Marshall et al., 2015).

Comparison and Contrast of Small Business Natural Disaster Success Factors

Many factors go into the survival of small businesses, such as infrastructure and indirect storm damage (Patankar & Patwardhan, 2016). Small business operating experience may serve as a survival factor in the aftermath of a natural disaster (Schrank et al., 2013). This section will include a comparison and contrast of how small business owners have survived the aftermath of natural disasters.

Internal and infrastructure damage to small businesses. Uninsured damages have had a profound effect on small business closures after a natural disaster (Patankar & Patwardhan, 2016). Indirect damage to the firm from storm events are not cover by hazard insurance. A gap exists in the literature between business closures and the indirect damages caused by natural disasters (Patankar & Patwardhan, 2016). Large corporations absorb disaster costs better that small firms because of the size compared to small businesses whose leaders likely have fewer resources at their disposal (Muñoz-Gómez, 2016).

In the aftermath of Hurricane Wilma in West Palm Beach, Florida, significant amounts of personal property damage suffered by business owners contributed to the length of time to recovery for their businesses (Atkinson & Sapat, 2014). Even with substantial resource infusion, South Florida small business leaders did not prevent natural disaster damage when they did not include planning (Sarmiento et al., 2015). Damage to a business was less of a factor in determining a company's ability to recover from a natural disaster than was a personal loss suffered by business owners in the aftermath (Atkinson & Sapat, 2014).

In a comparison by Patankar and Patwardhan (2016), indirect damage from natural disaster infrastructure damage was not significant towards small business closures. Leaders of small businesses need to work together with public governmental agencies by coordinating infrastructure undertakings through scenario planning (Baba et al., 2014). Much of the infrastructure in the private sector has limited access after a natural disaster, which may impede business customer flow (Schrank et al., 2013).

Customer retention and experience. A lack of access because of storm damage may limit some consumers' ability to patronize small businesses (Schrank et al., 2013). Doern (2016) noted that business leaders could help their businesses recover quickly after a disaster by offering customer discounts. In a survey conducted by Asgary et al. (2012), 26% of businesses' ability to recover from a natural disaster depended on customer retention. Business owners noted that devoted customers helped their businesses recover from Hurricane Sandy (Clay, Colburn, & Seara, 2016). In the aftermath, small business owners in businesses such as plant nurseries, roofing, plumbing, appliances and furnishing retained customers (Xiao & Nilawar, 2013).

In a study of 200 small business owners in Mississippi after Hurricane Katrina, the owners' experience and operating in the service industry were major success factors in surviving a natural disaster (Schrank et al., 2013). Older small businesses whose leaders had previous experienced natural disasters fared better younger small business, whose leaders did not have previous experience with natural disasters. A gap exists in the literature on the effect experience has on small business survival when comparing closed businesses to ones that remain open in the aftermath of a natural disaster (Schrank et al., 2013).

Views Related to Previous Research and Findings

The purpose of this qualitative case study was to explore how business owners in northeastern Florida avoided permanent business closure in the aftermath of a natural disaster. Increasing financial losses from natural disasters are forcing sole proprietors to collaborate more on finding mitigation solutions involving government programs such as FEMA and the SBA (Baba et al., 2014). More organizational leaders are employing risk–based strategies by building partnerships between business continuity and disaster recovery organizations (Epstein & Khan, 2014). Small business leaders can create disaster mitigation solutions by aligning their businesses with risk–reducing techniques and implementing company–wide natural disaster strategies (Baba et al., 2014). Private–public partnerships reduce costs and increase trust (Vinayagamoorthy, 2014). Similarly, legislative assistance reduces businesses' susceptibility to natural disasters by helping neutralize financial liability in the local small business population through private–public partnerships between local government and business (Atkinson & Sapat, 2014; Farazmand, 2014).

Radford, Senkbeil, and Rockman (2013) used both qualitative and quantitative analysis processes to study the effects of current graphics on assisting the public with information on imminent hurricanes. Radford et al. collected 166 completed surveys from Pensacola, Florida, and 149 completed surveys from Jacksonville, Florida. The findings indicated the cone of uncertainty has confused people trying to evacuate and make safety decisions. The cone of uncertainty indicates that hurricanes will likely take the track of the cone during a storm (Radford et al., 2013). Leaders of small businesses mostly operate their businesses from home or small properties (Schrank et al., 2013).

Transition and Summary

Section 1 included a discussion of several aspects of this study: (a) foundation of the study, (b) the background of the problem, (c) a general and specific statement of the problem, (d) the purpose statement, (e) the contextual nature of the study, (f) the research question, and (g) the open–ended interview questions. The purpose of this qualitative multiple case study was to explore what strategies business owners in northeastern Florida used to avoid permanent business closure in the aftermath of a natural disaster. The target population was small business owners in the retail and wholesale industry in northeastern Florida who avoided permanent business closure in the aftermath of a natural disaster. I functioned as the primary instrument of data collection, management, and analysis and maintained strict adherence to ethical guidelines. I also presented strategies that business leaders may find helpful when preparing for the aftermath of natural disasters that I discovered in the review of the professional and academic literature.

Section 2 will include details about the research project, purpose of the study, role of the researcher, participants, research method and design, population and sampling, and ethical research. In Section 2, I will also provide specifics related to data collection, including data collection instruments, data collection techniques, data organization techniques, and data analysis. I will also discuss reliability and validity, describe my plan to ensure the study would meet quality standards, and present a transition and summary in Section 2.

Section 3 of the research study will include an overview of the study. My discussions in Section 3 will include a presentation of the findings, applications to professional practice, and implications for social change. In Section 3, I will also present recommendations for further study, reflections learned during the doctoral study journey, and the conclusion.

Section 2: The Project

Section 2 will include a discussion of the study. The discussions in Section 2 will cover the purpose statement, my role as the researcher, the participants, the research method and design, the population sampling, and the research ethics. Data collection, data organization techniques, data analysis techniques, reliability, and validity, are additional topics I will discuss in the chapter, followed by the transition and summary. Section 3 will then include a brief overview of the study and a presentation of the findings.

Purpose Statement

The purpose of this qualitative multiple case study was to explore what strategies business owners in northeastern Florida used to avoid permanent business closure in the aftermath of a natural disaster. The target population was small business owners in the retail and wholesale industry in northeastern Florida who avoided permanent business closure in the aftermath of a natural disaster. The implications for positive social change include the potential for small business owners to address the potential for a natural disaster, maintain employment, and continue to have a positive effect on their community economically.

Role of the Researcher

A researcher's role is to function as the primary research instrument for data collection and to serve as the mediator of evidence by using multiple sources to collect data (Merriam & Tisdell, 2015; Yilmaz, 2013; Yin, 2014). As the researcher for this study, I conducted a qualitative multiple case study. I interviewed the participants, performed document analysis, coded data, identified patterns and themes, and drew conclusions. As the mediator of evidence, I included methodological data triangulation methods, such as interviews with semistructured questions, document analysis, member checking, a codebook, and a research log.

In qualitative research, it is necessary for researchers to clarify their role by explaining their relationship to the study topic or participants (Stake, 2010; Unluer, 2012). I had a personal and professional interest in discovering successful preparation and recovery strategies for small business owners following a natural disaster. As a firefighter, I helped limit the spread of existing or potential fires resulting from natural disasters. This knowledge and experience included dealing with hazardous material, providing medical care, transporting victims to hospitals, and performing searches and rescues. In retirement, I continue to search for natural disaster mitigation solutions for the community. Given the geographic location of the target population, my relationship to this study was also personal. The northeastern region of Florida is my home, so the study outcomes can benefit small business leaders in my community and neighboring communities.

Ethical Considerations

The ethical considerations associated with a study will enhance its credibility (Cartwright, Hickman, Nelson, & Knafl, 2013; Unluer, 2012), especially as my primary concern was to protect the rights of the study participants as described in the *Belmont Report*. First, I obtained permission to conduct this study from the Institutional Review Board (IRB) of Walden University before initiating this research. Next, I explained the informed consent process to the participants, making sure I did not target business owners that were still in a crisis. Before the interviews began, I obtained signed forms from each of the participants. The informed consent form included the nature and purpose of the study; an explanation of participants' confidentiality rights, which led to a determination of the participants' willingness to participate; and an explanation of data collection procedures, potential risks and benefits, data analysis, and data storage. The ethical considerations and methods included compliance with the university's guidelines and with the ethical principles outlined in the *Belmont Report*. Safeguarding the anonymity of participants is paramount (Cartwright et al., 2013; Mikesell, Bromley, & Khodyakov, 2013), and in the findings, I used pseudonyms to identify participants rather than names or other personally identifying information. Cartwright et al. (2013) and Mikesell et al. (2013) noted researchers should avoid sensitive topics and targeting vulnerable populations, such as minors, individuals with mental challenges, and inmates.

Bias

The confrontation of blind spots helps to eliminate researchers' prejudices (Unluer, 2012). Researchers can influence the data collection process, especially during interviews, by deeming information unimportant or irrelevant due to existing preconceived notions (Bulpitt & Martin, 2010; Yin, 2014). As a firefighter, I possess knowledge about the adverse effects of natural disasters on businesses, communities, and business continuity planning; therefore, it was necessary for me to monitor my body language and tone of voice during the interview process to avoid indicating my approval or disapproval with the participants' views. A researcher log includes any personal reflections or thoughts recorded by researchers (Williams, 2015). By acknowledging my biases, I improved the reliability and validity of the study.

Interview Protocol

Interview protocols consist of explaining to the participants what was going to happen, how it will happen, and why it was happening (Ariza, Lindeman, Mozumder & Suman, 2014). An interview protocol (see Appendix B) generated by a researcher ensures the consistency of interview questions (see Appendix C) across all interviewees (Lindström, 2012; Spaulding, 2014). Interview protocols consist of six to eight open–ended questions related to the phenomenon under study and help researchers to adopt an in-depth interviewing style to understand a phenomenon from the participants' point of view (Doody & Doody, 2015). The interview protocol was used to maintain consistency throughout the interview process.

Participants

Inclusionary criteria are necessary for research, especially when considering certain factors or conditions while selecting potential candidates and ensuring a fair sampling (Holloway & Wheeler, 2013). The eligibility requirements for participants in this study included small business owners that operated in the retail and wholesale business, regardless of gender or ethnicity, located in northeastern Florida. Only business owners who maintained business continuity after a natural disaster and possessed preparation and recovery strategies were eligible. All participants possessed knowledge related to surviving a natural disaster. In the study, I used convenience and purposeful sampling techniques to gain access to the population (Benoot, Hannes, & Bilsen, 2016; Dasgupta, 2015).

My initial contact with the participants took place via telephone. Initial contact is a researcher's first opportunity to bond with participants (Doykos, Brinkley-Rubinstein, Craven, McCormack, & Geller, 2014). Researchers share their identity with potential candidates regarding interdisciplinary training, background, and understanding of the study topic and ask them key questions related to the eligibility criteria (Doykos et al., 2014; Holloway & Wheeler, 2013). Researchers talk to potential participants about their willingness to participate in a study, and if they agree, researchers schedule a future interview date, time, and location (Miner-Romanoff, 2012). I thanked individuals who declined to participate or who were ineligible to participate. I briefly discussed with the participants who were identified as eligible, the potential benefits of the study's outcomes to gain new information on mitigating natural disaster events associated with business closures. Researchers try to strengthen their relationship with participants through subsequent contacts, as relationship development is critical for validating a study's eligibility criteria (Knight-Agarwal et al., 2015; McCrae, Blackstock, & Purssell, 2015; Pressler et al., 2012). I made additional contact with participants during the member checking follow–up interview.

Research Method and Design

Research Method

The three research methods are qualitative, quantitative, and mixed methods (Arghode, 2012; Makrakis & Kostoulas-Makrakis, 2016; Taber, 2012), and each approach has unique traits (Leedy & Ormrod, 2013). For example, quantitative research objectives involve testing study hypotheses for statistical significance, making comparisons between one or more groups, or making predictions (Arghode, 2012; Bezzina & Saunders, 2014; Taber, 2012). Quantitative research designs can be descriptive, comparative, correlational, and predictive (Bezzina & Saunders, 2014). In contrast, qualitative research is most appropriate for studies intended to explore and explain relatively new or ambiguous phenomena (Farrelly, 2013; Makrakis & Kostoulas-Makrakis, 2016; Taber, 2012). When using the qualitative approach, researchers study individuals, groups, or issues in depth in their natural setting; identify patterns and themes; and subsequently use them as the focal point to analyze contextual data (Barnham, 2012; Baškarada, 2014; Leedy & Ormrod, 2013; Yilmaz, 2013). A mixed methods approach (a combination of both quantitative and qualitative methods) was not ideal for this study, as the study did not include numerical data to test hypotheses (Landrum & Garza, 2015; Makrakis & Kostoulas-Makrakis, 2016; Stanimirovic & Vintar, 2015). I generated thick, rich descriptions rather than reported statistical data. Quantitative study variables included in mixed methods research do not always broaden the understanding of participants' perceptions, experiences, or beliefs explored in the qualitative side of a study design (Landrum & Garza, 2015; Makrakis & Kostoulas-Makrkis, 2016; Stanimirovic & Vintar, 2015). In this study, I explored the strategies that business owners in northeastern Florida used to avoid permanent business closure in the aftermath of a natural disaster and so the qualitative method was most appropriate.

Research Design

The qualitative design I chose for this study was a case study. Researchers use the case study design to obtain extensive knowledge about a phenomenon resulting from a real–life situation (Boblin, Ireland, Kirkpatrick, & Robertson, 2013; Stake, 2010; Stanimirovic & Vintar, 2015). There are different types of case studies, and selection of a design varies depending on the objective of the study or the research questions (Hancock & Algozzine, 2011; Merriam & Tisdell, 2015). Single–case studies are suitable to understand an individual or group associated with a phenomenon, and multiple case studies involve separate cases in which within–case analysis and across–case analysis also take place (Yin, 2014). Case studies can be exploratory, descriptive, explanatory, intrinsic, instrumental, or collective (Tsang, 2013; Yin, 2014).

I used a multiple case study research design to explore natural disaster solutions used by small business owners following a natural disaster. Researchers conduct multiple case studies to compare and contrast situations (Leedy & Ormrod, 2013; Webb, 2015). In this study, the participants explained how they survived the aftermath of a natural disaster through the interview process. Researchers use the interview process to gain different perceptions of issues participants faced (Leedy & Ormrod, 2013; Rudnick, 2014; Sinkovics & Alfoldi, 2012).

Other qualitative research designs did not apply to this study. The focus of the ethnographic design is whole cultures (Coughlin, 2013), which was not my intent with this study. The phenomenological research design was not suitable because the emphasis in this type of design is on the lived experience and perceptions of people (Bevan, 2014) rather than on exploring how people prepare and initiate plans.

Population and Sampling

Purposive sampling techniques are a nonprobability method of sampling because researchers intentionally select participants to fit the purpose of the study (Benoot et al., 2016; Emerson, 2015). A population sampling is a set of inclusion criteria or exclusion criteria, or a combination of both; that must be specified for the study (Robinson, 2014).The technique I selected for this study involved choosing suitable candidates who had experienced the phenomenon and could provide answers to the research question.

I initially contacted potential participants via telephone. I used paper phone books and digital listings to find small businesses in northeastern Florida. Asking fundamental questions regarding their experiences with natural disasters in a business continuity capacity following a natural disaster helped me to determine which individuals were eligible to participate. Researchers select participants who can provide multiple perspectives and a broad understanding of their perceptions and scope of practice (White, Oelke, & Friesen, 2012). Researchers should continue the inquiry process until data become redundant or repetitive or until no new information emerges (Fusch & Ness, 2015; Marshall, Cardon, Poddar, & Fontenot, 2013). Data saturation occurs through methodological data triangulation techniques, including interviews, audio recordings, document analysis, and member checking. Also, I obtained data saturation utilizing participants documents for analysis and the recurring themes.

Ethical Research

Respecting and protecting the rights of human subjects is the essential principle of research ethics (Frechtling & Boo, 2012; Greaney et al., 2012; Snyder, 2012). Before participant selection, I gave potential participants information regarding my study and the role of participants. Researchers take steps to ensure participants' autonomy by avoiding coercion, undue influence, and unnecessary harm (Bledsoe & Grizzle, 2013; Strause, 2013). I satisfied these ethical requirements in this study and will discuss the informed consent, participant anonymity, confidentiality rights, and options to withdraw that I used to do so in the following subsections.

Informed Consent

Using informed consent forms in research can be a gateway to building positive relationships with participants while revealing unknown aspects of a study (Bledsoe & Grizzle, 2013; Fassinger & Morrow, 2013; Owen, 2014). During the first telephone contact, individuals who agreed to the interview gave me verbal consent. I emailed each participant informed consent forms before conducting the interview. At the onset of the interview process, I acknowledged that participants had agreed to participate. The individuals were also able to ask questions of me, if necessary. I informed the individuals of the time needed to participate and explained why I asked them to take part in the study.

Pseudonyms. Researchers often use pseudonyms known only to the researchers instead of participants' names (Hancock & Algozzine, 2011; Miles, Huberman, & Saldaña, 2014). I generated pseudonyms (e.g., Participant 1, Participant 2, etc.) to identify each participant within the data collected, including on the informed consent forms, audio recordings, transcribed interviews, and data analysis. Potential participants had the opportunity to read the contents of the informed consent form and to indicate that they voluntarily agreed to participate or declined to participate in this study by checking a box (see Appendix C). I kept the completed informed consent agreements, but the participants could receive a copy upon request.

Confidentiality. Researchers take precautions with data by keeping them in a secure location (Leedy & Ormrod, 2013). Dropbox is a computer storage company that protects data files with software encryption and firewalls (Latha, Gowsalya, & Kannega, 2014). I secured the data files in an online data storage system equipped with password and user identification. A third party transcribed the information but did not know the identities of the voices on the audio recordings. I coded the actual identifiers created for each participant. The data remained in my possession until I uploaded the data to the online Dropbox location, where it will stay for 5 years to safeguard the confidentiality rights of the participants.

Option to Withdraw

In compliance with the ethical principles of research, researchers explain participants' right to withdraw from a study at any time without hindrance or fear (Bellone, Navarick, & Mendoza, 2012; Frechtling & Boo, 2012; Van Wijk, 2014). Every 15 minutes throughout the interview process, I asked the participants if they were still comfortable answering interview questions and if they would like to continue. This process allowed the participants to express any discomfort and reminded them of their option to cease involvement at any time. Participants had the right to withdraw at any time without penalty. The responses from participants who prematurely withdraw were not part of the data analysis.

Study Incentives

Participation incentives may cause individuals to feel pressure to join a study for the incentives (Perez, Nie, Ardern, Radhu, & Ritvo, 2013). However, incentives may only have a small impact on participant recruitment efforts or retention rates while adding to the research expenses (Sánchez-Fernández, Muñoz-Leiva, & Montoro-Ríos, 2012). I mitigated any risks of exercising influence over the study participants, which included minimizing research costs. This study included no incentive to participate.

Data Collection

I was the data collection instrument in this qualitative study. I conducted semistructured interviews containing open–ended questions to obtain in-depth robust responses. I also built flexibility into the processes of collecting and presenting the analysis of the data by acting as the instrument.

Instruments

As the qualitative researcher, I was the primary instrument used to accumulate data (Houghton, Casey, Shaw, & Murphy, 2013; Kennedy-Clark, 2013). The primary data source was interviews with five small business owners. Case study data collection requires multiple resources for gathering data (Bang, 2012; Yin, 2014). I created an interview protocol to ensure consistency throughout the process of capturing business leaders' experiences and perceptions related to their business surviving a natural disaster (see Appendix B).

Participants provide input on the accuracy of the data collected through member checking (Marshall & Rossman, 2016). The basis of the semistructured questions was to understand how small business owners in northeastern Florida avoided permanent business closure in the aftermath of a natural disaster (see Appendix C). A member-checking process consists of performing an interview, recording what a participant says, sharing the data with the participant for accuracy, and validating that the emerging themes are consistent with the participant's intended description of events (Marshall & Rossman, 2016; Patton, 2015; Strauss & Corbin, 2015). The member–checking process enhances the reliability and validity of the data collection instrument.

Data Collection Technique

Data collection is an integral part of the research process for gathering information to answer research questions (Bang, 2012). Some researchers include several types of data collection methods in qualitative research (Bang, 2012; Yin, 2014). Interviews are suitable when exploring the perceptions or experiences of a phenomenon to establish meaning and understanding (Englander, 2012; Fusch & Ness, 2015). I used an audio-recording device in conjunction with the interview process, as this technique may enhance the quality of the study. Researchers use document analysis for deeper meaning or for reflecting specific social or historical conditions, circumstances, and situations (Miller & Alvarado, 2005; Yin, 2012). In addition to interviews, I analyzed the disaster readiness plans that were in place during the catastrophe, as well as the current plan. Researchers use methodological data triangulation to establish the quality and rigor of a study with the application of multiple data sources (Denzin & Lincoln, 2011; Heale & Forbes, 2013; Marshall & Rossman, 2016).

Interview Process

I began each interview with a brief discussion in which the participant acknowledged his or her willingness to participate. As recommended by Taubman, Leaf, McEachin, Papovich, and Leaf (2013), researchers should ask participants during the interview process if they fully understand the nature and purpose of the research to ensure accuracy. I provided time to ask questions or receive clarification about the study, and I reminded the participants that an audio device would record their responses to the interview questions before I activated the recording apparatus. Next, I asked the seven semistructured, open–ended questions listed on the interview protocol related to uncovering how business owners avoid business closure in the small business sector (see Appendix C). The main benefit of using the interview process is the ability to use follow–up or probing questions to obtain a deeper, richer description; to gain more details; or until data saturation achievement (Doody & Doody, 2015; Fusch & Ness, 2015; Merriam & Tisdell, 2015).

An advantage of conducting qualitative research is the production of rich, robust information that readers can understand (Patton, 2015). Research often has an aspect of the unknown, and the elasticity of qualitative research provides a better fit (Ritchie, Lewis, McNaughton, & Ormston, 2013). Qualitative data can transcend time and space and can allow readers to imagine what it would be like to have experienced the situation

(Patton, 2015). Disadvantages of qualitative data include the physical, intimidating presence or bias of a researcher (Marshall & Rossman, 2016).

Audio-Recording Device

Using audio–or video–recording devices during the interview process is a relatively common practice in research, and recording devices capture the entire viewpoint of the participants (Al-Yateem, 2012; Baškarada, 2014). To guard against any conflict, I informed the participants that I would use an audio recorder during the interview. I explained to the participants ahead of time that I would start and stop the audio–recording device for the interview. After discussing informed consent, I informed the participants that I was enabling the device, and then I initiated the interview process. When the interview process was over, I notified the participants when device deactivation occurred, and I no longer recorded their responses.

I downloaded the data from the audio–recording device into a password–protected computer and uploaded the audio interviews to a third party for transcription. Within 72 hours, I retrieved the transcribed interview files from my computer and proceeded to print the individual documents. It was necessary to perform cross–referencing techniques to verify the accuracy of the transcribed interviews and to execute the member–checking process. Transcribing interviews verbatim reduces the likelihood of omitting or misinterpreting participants' responses (Miles et al., 2014; Webber & Jones, 2013). Drawbacks associated with using audio–recording devices include inadvertently deleting audio data and storing audio files due to their potentially large size (Johnson, Dunlap, & Benoit, 2010).

Document analysis

Researchers should mostly obtain data by interviewing and surveying people and by reviewing documents (Owen, 2014). An analysis of documents can provide useful background information about a study topic and can benefit a researcher before the interview process (Miller & Alvarado, 2005; Owen, 2014). In this study, I reviewed existing disaster relief policies used during natural disasters and reviewed newspaper articles and other published works about recovery from a natural disaster. The accurate analysis helped to improve my authenticity as a researcher by demonstrating knowledge about the study phenomenon, enhancing communications, and strengthening relationships with the participants.

I also looked for opportunities to analyze documents that could further substantiate the strategies given by the participants. My primary interest was in the following document types: original disaster plans, strategic plans, business continuity plans, and standard operating procedures. Before concluding each interview, I asked the participants to share these documents, if applicable. All available documents underwent a review to identify relevant materials related to the phenomenon, and I asked follow–up questions to gain richer insight or understanding. The limitations associated with this technique include the time–consuming process of sifting through materials and filtering out old documents that are situational rather than permanent (Miller & Alvarado, 2005; Owen, 2014).

Member Checking

One way researchers create reliability is through member checking, which serves to guarantee credibility through participants' verification of the data collected during the interview and validating that the emerging themes are consistent with the participants' intended description of events (Reilly, 2013). The credibility of qualitative studies depends on the extent of rich, in–depth descriptions provided by the researcher (Simpson & Quigley, 2016; Yilmaz, 2013). Researchers establish credibility by sharing the approaches used to obtain their insight with participants (Harvey, 2015; Simpson & Quigley, 2016; Yu et al., 2013).

Data Organization Techniques

Organizing and documenting the data collected in case studies involve providing proof of information and the researcher's analysis (Yin, 2014). Contextual data or words can be difficult to structure and organize, so a variety of data organization techniques may be necessary (Johnson et al., 2010). Some organizational data systems include literature review maps, interviews, annotated notes, consent forms, and document request letters (Yin, 2014). I tracked and structured data using the following data organization techniques: audio–recorded and transcribed interviews, documents, a codebook, a research log, and Atlas.ti software.

Methodological data triangulation involves using data collected from multiple sources or respondents to shape and monitor the information obtained (Miles et al., 2014). Grouping data together involved downloading digital voice recordings of the participants' responses to interview questions to a password–protected computer. I received the transcribed interviews within 72 hours. In the research log, I noted any issues that I found when cross–referencing the audio recordings and the transcribed interviews. Researchers note any problems or concerns raised by the participants during the member-checking process (Stake, 2010).

I used a codebook, Atlas.ti software, and a research log to organize and track the evidence to support the analysis of data. Open coding was suitable to code the transcribed interviews and documents, and Atlas.ti software helped to generate themes and store data. A codebook displays word frequencies, which can lead to the categories that form themes (Ivey, 2015). Researchers use research logs to write down problems they experience with the data analysis or issues that arise from member checking the data (Williams, 2015).

Both the computer and paper formats of the data will remain in a secured location for 5 years. A flash drive will contain all interview audio recordings before I permanently delete the files from the hard disk of my personal computer. Researchers safely store data (e.g., consent forms, transcribed interviews, documents, codebooks, and research logs) in a location to which they have the only key (Ruivo, Santos, & Oliveira, 2014). After 5 years, I will destroy the flash drive by breaking it, and I will shred the paper-based data to protect the confidentiality of the participants and to comply with the university's research ethics guidelines.

Data Analysis Technique

I explored what strategies business owners in northeastern Florida used to avoid permanent business closure in the aftermath of a natural disaster. During natural disaster recovery, all stakeholders should have an interest in the marketing message (Mair,

Ritchie, & Walters, 2016). The intent of data analysis is to discover answers to a research question by gathering data from multiple sources (Carter, Bryant-Lukosius, DiCenso, Blythe, & Neville, 2014; Leedy & Ormrod, 2013). I used a five–stage data analysis process in this study. Data analysis can involve the following steps: (a) collecting data, (b) separating data into groups through coding, (c) grouping data into themes, (d) assessing the theme material, (e) and developing conclusions (Yin, 2012). I considered the theoretical implications involved in interpreting the findings regarding the conceptual framework and research question. I included a critical, retrospective examination of the framework presented in the literature review to consider new findings. I explained my consideration of the disconfirming evidence, counterexamples, or viable alternative interpretations and remained open to the possibility that other theoretical frameworks could have led to a better understanding of the problem.

The input was the raw data retrieved during the data collection phase, which included interviews, audio recordings, and document analysis. I verified transcribed data by cross–referencing the data with the audio recordings to ensure accuracy and noting inconsistencies. I asked participants to review the transcript and my interpretation of their responses for accuracy. Following the member–checking process, data underwent coding and further theme development.

Coding

Some coding techniques used to analyze contextual data involve iterative and incremental analysis at various stages (Arendt et al., 2012; Baškarada, 2014; Glaser & Laudel, 2013). In this study, open–coding techniques were suitable to structure the transcribed interviews and documents. Within the transcribed interviews, I looked for recurring words, phrases, or sentences to form categories regarding their relevance to the research questions. Researchers use assigned document tags, labels, or other indicators to highlight different segments of relevant text (Dasgupta, 2015). Researchers should keep all identified categories and themes in a codebook (Ivey, 2015). Keyword frequencies assist researchers in formulating themes that uncover successful preparation and recovery strategies perceived and experienced by business leaders following a natural disaster in small business sectors (Baškarada, 2014; Borrego, Foster, & Froyd, 2014; Glaser & Laudel, 2013).

Discovering Emergent Themes

Theme development should occur without manipulation or bias by a researcher (Dasgupta, 2015). Therefore, I took additional steps to ensure theme development happened more naturally. After manually coding transcribed interviews and documents, researchers can use iterative tests in Atlas.ti software to complete the process (Houghton et al., 2013). This content analysis software is suitable for theme development because data processing involves retrieving themes from audio or coded interview data and document data (Woods, Paulus, Atkins, & Macklin, 2015). Iterative tests first took place using each participant's responses to observe the themes that emerged. Next, I used the same coding with all five participants to see if emergent themes replicated the data analysis results of each participant and to see if new data surfaced. If there is no new information after coding, data saturation has occurred (Fusch & Ness, 2015).

Reporting Case Study Research

Researchers present findings of case studies in many ways (Remenyi, 2013; Yin, 2014). As the foundational inquiry was to discover how some business owners in northeastern Florida avoided permanent business closure in the aftermath of a natural disaster, I provided a thick, rich description of their experiences with natural disasters and the strategies they employed to ensure business continuity. It is not necessary to report every detail, but only the most relevant information as it relates to the phenomenon studied (Remenyi, 2013). I obtained relevant data related to this study using a narrative approach to discuss the participants' natural disaster experiences. I also summarized data from the transcribed interviews and documents that emphasized the participants recommended disaster relief preparation and recovery strategies. I used Atlas.ti for the data analysis to help manage the data and develop themes from the data collected. The qualitative software is a tool used to organize, store, code, and manage collected data, which improves research dependability (Pfaff et al., 2014).

Reliability and Validity

Major components of any research include the reliability and validity of the findings (Yin, 2012). Qualitative researchers' role is paramount in establishing quality and rigor by detailing their use of strategies to achieve credibility, dependability, confirmability, and transferability (Houghton et al., 2013; Miles et al., 2014; Peyrovi, Raiesdana, & Mehrdad, 2014). In the following subsections, I will describe how I achieved validity and reliability.

Credibility

In this study, credibility occurred through member checking. The credibility of qualitative research depends on the depth to which the results are believable and trustworthy (Klenke, 2016). Researchers must have a variety of strategies to ensure data credibility, such as debriefing, member checking, triangulation, or using a reflective journal (Carter et al., 2014; Yang & Wu, 2014). I recorded the interviews using an audio-recording device to ensure the accuracy of the transcribed interviews. As a third party transcribed the interviews, I read the transcribed interview and ensured credibility by asking participants to check the transcription for accuracy as a cross–referencing technique and validated that the emerging themes were consistent with each participant's intended description of the experience.

Dependability

Verifying data analysis results by asking participants to review the themes and the accuracy of findings is a means to achieve research dependability (Colbert, Wyatt–Smith, & Klenowski, 2012; Klenke, 2016). Researchers also use triangulation to establish dependability (Merriam & Tisdell, 2015; White et al., 2012). I provided details of the study procedures. I also kept an audit trail of the study and a research log of the data collection instruments, processes, and techniques, as well as methods for data coding, analysis, and interpretation. Independent investigators can use the audit trail to retrace their procedures quickly in the event of research replication.

Confirmability

The confirmability of qualitative research refers to the extent to which the results are verifiable by others regarding readability, objectivity, and credibility (Klenke, 2016;

Miles et al., 2014; Yin, 2014). Researchers can verify a study using a reflective journal or an audit trail that consists of raw data, analysis notes, process notes, and personal notes (Williams, 2015). I used an audit trail to generate a description of the data collection, coding process and codebook, data analysis procedures, and any issues that I experienced during the research study. I minimized researcher bias by using an interview protocol and bracketing or setting aside my personal assumptions and beliefs about the phenomenon studied to examine how the phenomenon appeared to the participants.

Transferability

Transferability or portability of qualitative research refers to the extent to which the findings apply to other contexts or settings to establish validity (Houghton et al., 2013; Klenke, 2016; Yilmaz, 2013). To strengthen validity, qualitative researchers frequently compare the rich, thick description of the findings (Houghton et al., 2013; Merriam & Tisdell, 2015). By linking the TPB to its practical application as it relates to the study phenomenon, I enhanced the transferability of the study findings to other small sector business leaders. However, researchers always leave transferability to the reader to decide (Marshall & Rossman, 2016; Porte, 2013).

The content validity of qualitative research results occurs through data saturation, but there are no set criteria for reaching content validity (Fusch & Ness, 2015). Some researchers have noted that data saturation occurs when there are sufficient data to replicate the study, whereas others contend the absence of new information, codes, or themes is an indication that data saturation has occurred (Fusch & Ness, 2015; O'Reilly & Parker, 2013). Data saturation does not take place when researchers have exhausted all their resources, but it occurs based on the depth of the data collected (Burmeister &

Aitken, 2012). I achieved data saturation when there was no new information on the

themes derived from the interviews, member checking, and document analysis process. I

also used follow–up questions to reach data saturation. The open–coding techniques and

Atlas.ti software helped to identify high–frequency words or phrases for theme

generation. Audit trails follow researchers' path using codebooks and research logs until

no new information is available (Walker, 2012).

Transition and Summary

Section 2 included the design, methodology, and data collection procedures for

the study, including information about my role as the researcher, ethical considerations in

research with human subjects, and the use of organizational data systems. Researchers

establish the quality of a study through ensuring reliability (credibility and dependability)

and validity (transferability and confirmability; Houghton et al., 2013; Yin, 2012). This

section concluded with a discussion on how I asked business owners to discuss how they

avoided business closure after a natural disaster.

Section 3 will include the detailed findings of the research study, as well as my

suggestions for future research. I will focus on how some business owners in northeastern

Florida avoided permanent business closure in the aftermath of a natural disaster. In

Section 3, I will also present the application of professional practice and implications for

social change.

Section 3: Application to Professional Practice and Implications for Change

The content of this section will include (a) an overview of the study, (b) the presentation of the findings, (c) applications to professional practice, (d) implications for social change, and (e) recommendations for action. The remaining subsections will be recommendations for further studies, reflections, and the summary and conclusion. In Section 3, I will also provide a discussion on how study themes relate to the conceptual frameworks and the findings.

Overview of Study

The purpose of this qualitative multiple case study was to explore what strategies small business owners in northeastern Florida use to avoid permanent business closure in the aftermath of a natural disaster. The study population consisted of small business owners in the retail and wholesale industry who had survived a natural disaster in northeastern Florida. The findings revealed small business owners who survived after a natural disaster had a positive attitude and took control in the aftermath of the natural disaster. Altay et al. (2013) contended that when business owners deciding to plan for a natural disaster, the use of TPB, having a positive attitude, adhering to norms, and maintaining perceived control were critical. Participants in this study noted that what mattered most to business owners was their VI or stake in surviving the aftermath of natural disasters. Conversely, Adame and Miller (2016) indicated that VI is necessary when preparing for disasters.

Presentation of the Findings

The overarching research question guiding this study was as follows: What strategies do small business owners use to avoid permanent business closure in the aftermath of a natural disaster? The case study design included data from two sources. The primary source of data was in–depth interviews with five small business owners in northeastern Florida. I also reviewed documents related to the participants' disaster readiness planning. My review of peer-reviewed journals served as the groundwork to connect the research question with the theoretical framework to provide a robust source of secondary data.

The study sample for this qualitative multiple case study consisted of five small business owners in the retail and wholesale industry in northeastern Florida. I used pseudonyms (e.g., Participant 1, Participant 2, etc.) to preserve the confidentiality of the participants. Demographic data from the small business owners who survived the adverse effects of a natural catastrophe appear in Table 2. Four participants (80%) were retail business owners, and one participant (20%) was a commercial business owner. The participants' years of business experience ranged from 11 years to 43 years. Three participants (60%) were male, and two (40%) were female. The average interview time was 20 minutes 17 seconds.

Table 2

Demographic Data for Owners of Small Businesses That Survived a Natural Disaster

Participant	Position or title	Location	Years of business experience
P1	Business owner	Florida	40
P2	Business owner	Florida	30
P3	Business owner	Florida	15
P4	Business owner	Florida	11
P5	Business owner	Florida	43

The semistructured questions that I developed and incorporated into the interview protocol included the same seven questions presented to every participant. Some participants did not maintain preparedness and recovery plans. Using interviews, documents, and member checking revealed holistic and robust strategies the small business owners had used for the survival of their business after a natural disaster. I will discuss key elements of the study in the following subsections.

A Review of the Thematic Creation

In the semistructured interviews, the participants responded to my seven open–ended questions and provided an in–depth understanding of how business owners in northeastern Florida avoided permanent business closure in the aftermath of a natural disaster. I analyzed each participant's response to each interview question separately and coded it for the recurring themes. I then conducted a second analysis using all of the participant responses combined. The same major themes resulted from this analysis as the first. The major themes were (a) flood barriers, (b) maintaining adequate insurance coverage, (c) damage and destruction aftermath, and (d) planning experience.

The most common phase was flooding because of the damaging effects in the wake of a natural disaster. Experience with natural disaster planning may be a key to surviving in the aftermath of a natural catastrophe. The most common keyword

developmental phases from the data analysis appear in Table 3.

Table 3

Code Frequency

Codes	*n*	Theme
Strategy: Preventive use of sandbags	21	1, 3
Strategy: Planning experience	24	1, 4
Strategy: Flood insurance	18	2, 3
Strategy: Preventing damage	16	3
Strategy: Using foam spray at the entrance and exit	10	3
Strategy: Immediate response	9	4

I also conducted another analysis that included a most common code word count.

Grouping code words allowed me to build theme relationships. Participants' secondary

word grouping led to theoretical ideas. The keywords presented in Table 4 comprise

theoretical ideas that resulted in thematic formation.

Table 4

Top Seven Frequently Occurring Words and Groups Related to Content and Context

No.	Groups and keywords	Theoretic ideas	Theme	*n*
1	Planning experience	No experience	4	35
2	Insurance	Avoid business closure	2	28
3	Flood barriers	Mitigation strategies	3	24
4	Norms, attitudes, and responses	Recover as soon as possible	4	15
5	Self-efficacy	Immediacy	1	11
6	Damage and destruction	Lift merchandise	3	27
7	Strategies businesses may enact	Protect entrances and exits	1	5

Note. See Table D1 for breakdown by the participant.

The participants indicated that protective barriers enhanced long–term survival in

the aftermath of natural disasters, especially in northeastern Florida because of the high

incidence of flood–related catastrophes. The participants also noted that in the wake of catastrophes, their focus was on maintaining business operations. The coded frequency

by the participants for Themes 1 through 4 appear in Table 5.

Table 5

Subjects Mentioned Most Frequently by Participants

	P1	P2	P3	P4	P5	Frequency	Theme
Planning experience	Y	Y		Y	Y	4	4
Insurance	Y	Y	Y	Y	Y	5	2
Lifting merchandise off the floor	Y	Y	Y			3	3
Response aftermath	Y	Y	Y	Y	Y	5	3
Immediacy	Y	Y		Y	Y	4	3
Flood barriers	Y	Y	Y			3	1
Building damage	Y	Y	Y	Y	Y	5	3

Theme 1: Flood Barriers

Participant 1 (P1) indicated sandbag barriers erected at the front and back

entrances of the business assisted in surviving Hurricane Matthew. P1 also described how

spray foam prevented floodwaters from entering the business during Hurricane Matthew.

Chinh, Bubeck, Dung, and Kreibich (2016) suggested the use of protective barriers would

help with flood prevention. Chinh et al. also contended that some businesses refused to

purchase flood barriers for extreme weather events because of cost. Participant 2 (P2)

also erected concrete barrier walls around the business to keep out floodwaters.

Participant 3 (P3) stated that the use of sandbags as a floodwater preventive measure was

effective in preparation for Hurricane Matthew. P3's business may have survived because

the business owner operated an additional store away from the disaster zone that doubled

as a storage facility during Hurricane Matthew. The coded frequency of Theme 1 appears

in Table 6.

Table 6

Theme 1 Analysis

Code frequency	Word frequency	Participant frequency
21 (Flood barriers)	24	3

Business owners who took extra protection were able to reopen after minor cleanup tasks such as tree removal and utility restoration. P1, P2, and P3 noted that sandbags or concrete walls helped their businesses survive by protecting their assets in the wake of Hurricane Matthew. The placing of temporary barriers, such as sandbags, at the front and back doors were key strategic tasks put in place before natural disaster strikes. Daramola et al. (2016) suggested that natural disaster adaptive strategies could serve as disaster–reducing strategies. P2 elaborated on having permanent flood barrier walls and local agency assistance in the aftermath. The disaster preparedness of P1, P2, P3, and P4 demonstrated planned behavior and VI relating to the conceptual frameworks used in this study.

Theme 2: Maintaining Adequate Insurance Coverage

Participant 5 (P5) explained that although a person cannot prevent natural disasters, having the right type of insurance is important. Insurance agents who understand business needs may prevent business closure. Herbane (2013) noted business owners understand the negative impact disasters have on their business, and the owners purchase business interruption insurance to mitigate this effect. P5's business suffered natural disaster damages totaling $55,000. Sarmiento et al. (2015) noted business owners do not understand the impact natural disasters have on their long- and short-term stability and resources. P3 did not have flood insurance, even though the business was two blocks from a major waterway. Northeastern Florida small business owners who maintain adequate insurance coverage make an investment in the business future.

Also, P3 mentioned that the company's insurance broker never suggested purchasing flood insurance. Some participants liked knowing about the various forms of disaster insurance coverage available. The coded frequency of Theme 2 appears in Table 7.

Table 7

Theme 2 Analysis

Code frequency	Word frequency	Participant frequency
18 (Insurance)	28	5

The views of P3 and P4 on insurance contrasted with research that indicated disaster insurance coverage prevented business closure in the aftermath of a natural disaster. Neither P4, before a fire destroyed the company's business, or P3 before Hurricane Matthew destroyed the business, carried disaster insurance. P3 stated that they would purchase flood insurance for future natural disasters. De Mel et al. (2012) contended that a lack of business disaster insurance negatively affects the ability of small businesses to recover. Pathak and Ahmad (2016) noted insurance is not the only factor involved in disaster recovery, as disaster mitigation and preparedness are crucial in the aftermath. Chinh et al. (2016) contended that flood insurance, early warning systems, and cash reserves might prevent business failure related to natural catastrophes.

The time lag between a natural disaster and the insurance adjuster's arrival was too long in some cases. Participants used friends, family, and cash reserves to maintain business continuity until insurance coverage and other disaster relief arrived. These findings are significant for current small business owners and new business owners because they provide practical lessons learned from natural disaster planning. After their experience with natural disasters, all the participants considered a planned behavior of purchasing business insurance was a key component of their experience with catastrophes.

Theme 3: Damage and Destruction Aftermath

P1's business suffered $12,000 in damage and destruction from Hurricane Matthew. Participant 1 also noted local code regulations prevented raising the electrical outlets during the repairs after the disaster. Poussin, Wouter Botzen, and Aerts, (2015) contended that raising the electrical outlets provided more basic protection from flooding than concrete or waterproof floors. P3 used $12,000 in cash reserves to repair the damage and destruction to their merchandise and wrote off $13,000 of merchandise as a tax loss. P1, P2, and P3 all described lifting merchandise off the floor to prevent damage from floodwaters.

P5 wholesale business suffered complete destruction from a tornado. Asgary et al. (2012) noted that difficult roads and other infrastructure damage and destruction might contribute to business closure. P2 described how coordinating with local officials restored utility systems such as lights and water. Businesses that can avoid high levels of disruption and significant building damage after a natural catastrophe may have a better chance of surviving (Kousky, 2014). P1 also noted that Hurricane Matthew caused equipment damage and required equipment rental. Alternatively, Filatova (2014) contended that a positive behavior change of carrying insurance or waterproofing a business might reduce natural disaster damaging effects on small businesses. The coded

frequency of Theme 3 appears in Table 8.

Table 8

Theme 3 Analysis

Code frequency	Word frequency	Participant frequency
16 (Damage and destruction)	27	5

P4 described how a natural disaster damaged the business floor and 10 to 15

pieces of clothing. The main damage was to the flooring, which caused temporary

business closure for a week. P1 described how the floodwaters came through the doors,

which caused electrical and wall damage and caused temporary business closure for 30

days. P2 explained how the downed trees in the wake of Hurricane Matthew caused

indirect damage to their uncovered parking lot.

P3 suffered $25,000 in building and merchandise damage and destruction from

Hurricane Matthew. Business owners may not be able to enter their businesses after a

natural disaster to assess damage and destruction (Lin et al., 2014). P4 stated local

officials were unclear on the timetable for reentry to their businesses. Some business

owners may be allowed reentry for a fixed period to assess the damage (Siebeneck,

Lindell, Prater, Wu, & Huang, 2012). Participants feared mounting natural disaster

damage, as well as damage and destruction from looters. P1, 2, 3, 4, and 5 incurred

damage and destruction from natural catastrophes.

Theme 4: Experience with Natural Disasters

Business owner P1 noted that natural disaster lessons learned assisted in

developing a disaster plan. Catastrophe experience is a critical factor in predicting future outcomes of natural disasters (Guo & Li, 2016). P2 stated that experience was a crucial factor in preparing for the aftereffects of Hurricane Matthew. P3 stated Hurricane Matthew was a learning experience and that not having flood insurance could have caused business failure. Asgary (2012) noted that younger business owners were less likely to be successful than older, more experienced owners. Participants who experienced natural disasters may have a better chance of surviving future natural disasters. The coded frequency for Theme 4 appears in Table 9.

Table 9

Theme 4 Analysis

Code frequency	Word frequency	Participant frequency
24 (Experience)	35	4

P4 has been in business for 11 years, but never experienced a natural disaster. Participant 4 had an unwritten plan that called for shuttering up windows and using sandbags at the doors to prevent flooding. Cameron and Shah (2015) noted the wake of a natural disaster makes a person more risk averse than if they never experienced a natural disaster. A major natural disaster has not directly hit the northeastern Florida region since Hurricane Dora in 1964. As a result, businesses in northeastern Florida may lack natural disaster experience. P3 had no experience planning for natural disasters but survived the natural catastrophe. Schrank et al. (2013) noted that using disaster experience as a strategy may not prevent closure if business owners make bad business decisions before a natural catastrophe.

P5's experience with disasters was a key factor in developing a disaster plan. Participant 2 stated past disaster encounters prepared the business for future natural disasters. Izumi and Shaw (2014) noted that business owners who had suffered a natural disaster were more likely to adopt a natural disaster plan.

Analysis of TPB Theory Related to the Findings

Business owners' behaviors related to surviving the aftermath of natural disasters. These components were norms, response, and perceived behavioral control. Attitude, norms, and response determined the amount of storm damage and other post–disaster problems such as customer retention and employee retention. This section will include (a) business owners' response in the aftermath of a natural disaster, (b) business owners perceived control, and (c) business owners' attitude and intention related to natural disasters prevention.

Business Owners' Response in the Aftermath

Some Participants response in the wake of Hurricane Matthew involved working 21 straight days to prepare to reopen. Mancha and Yoder (2015) noted that peer beliefs, assumed control, and attitude makes a difference when preparing for the aftermath of a catastrophe. P2 response in the wake of a natural disaster was to reopen as soon as possible after the natural disaster. A response behavioral concern after natural disasters were the downed trees and power outages. In contrast, Sniehotta, Presseau, and Araújo-Soares (2014) noted that using (TPB) to explain human behavior was not empirically valid. Planned behavior does not always lead to practical results. P3 responded to Hurricane Matthew by relocating merchandise away from the area.

Participants noted that the aftermath response behavior of rival businesses was to prove a temporary location and telephone system communication for the company. Also,

P5 noted the response after the tornado was to make sure customers and suppliers were aware of their current business circumstances. Also, participants stated that during the catastrophe, cell phones were used to order supplies and take customer orders. P1, 2, 3, 4, and 5 noted the primary natural disaster response was to begin business operations in the aftermath of the natural disaster.

Business Owner Perceived Control

Perceived control was a critical behavior demonstrated by the small business owners. Ayala and Manzano (2014) noted that a major part of control depended on the amount resourcefulness and the individual's belief in the outcome of the situation. Participants noted that perceived control was largely related to flood barriers that prevented reduced flooding of the businesses. Sánchez–Medina et al. (2014) indicated natural disaster preparedness perceived control intentions depended on the difficulty perceived by the owner. Participants whose businesses were close to a waterway described how proximity to the waterway reduced the perceived control of surviving natural disasters.

Participants felt confident they would overcome the adverse effects of the natural disaster experience. Resiliency, flood insurance, family, friends, and community support enhanced their perceived control. In addition to perceived control business owners' norms and attitudes are critical in surviving catastrophes.

Business Owners' Norms and Attitudes

Participants' disaster preparedness norms and attitudes were varied. P1, 2, and 4 were proactive. Johnson et al. (2014) contended that attitude toward any given situation depended on how much was at risk. In contrast, Chen (2016) indicated that an extended version of TPB, in addition to norms and attitude, should include one's moral obligation in reducing the adverse effects of natural disasters on business and society. Participants' attitude focused on preparing to reopen as soon as possible after the catastrophe. Contrastingly, P2 noted that the business norm was preparing for natural disasters because of the proximity of the business to the river. Business owners' intentional disaster preparation, whether written or memorized, played a vital role in avoiding permanent business closure in the natural disaster aftermath. The businesses of those participants who either intentionally or unintentionally did not plan for a natural disaster survived due to responding with urgency and having an attitude of resiliency.

Participants noted that positive response of employees was an important factor in the wake of the natural disaster. Adame and Miller (2015) contended that preparing for a natural disaster required the antecedents' attitude, norms, and perceived control to produce specific behavioral outcomes. P3's attitudes regarding natural disaster preparedness did not consist of a written disaster emergency plan. Alternatively, Ajzen and Sheikh (2013) noted the variables used in TPB were not necessary to produce intentions and perceptions. Adame and Miller (2015) noted that resource accessibility and relevance must take place when developing disaster planning attitudes. Interestingly, P3 refused to develop a written natural disaster plan for future catastrophes even though the business suffered major damage as a result of Hurricane Matthew.

Analysis of VI Theory Related to the Findings

Business owners believed self–efficacy or confidence contributed to their ability to maintain business continuity and empowered their employees, family, and community. Ajzen (1985) noted new information might not be enough to sway individuals' intentions if they are confident in what they believe. Small business owners' self–efficacy or confidence in surviving the aftermath of a natural disaster included a focus on cognitive aspects associated with natural disaster preparedness and recovery. Participants used three primary factors related to their VI in surviving natural disasters in northeastern Florida: (a) business owner's stake in disaster planning, (b) belief in their ability to survive in the aftermath, (c) and the immediacy action behavior of the business owners related to natural disasters.

Business Owner Stake in Disaster Planning

Participants' VI dominant response focused on the financial stake in the firm. P1 had a 30–year financial stake in the business. Adame and Miller (2016) noted business owners' stake placed a subjective value on what is important. In contrast, Johnson et al. (2014) indicated that a person's stake is different from ego–driven feelings about a situation. Participants noted that planning mistakes included not preparing enough for the floodwaters and not moving the computers, merchandise, and relevant documents at least two feet off the ground before the natural disaster strike. P4 and 5 noted it was not just the business at stake, but employees and the community's survival.

Certainty and the Ability to Survive the Aftermath

Participants had no doubt about surviving the natural disaster. Adame and Miller (2016) noted that being certain was a major component in the VI decision–making process. Miller et al. (2013) noted certainty is the consequential essence of behavior related to an attitude. P1 demonstrated behavioral certainty by remaining in the business for 21 making sure the business would reopen after the natural disaster. Participants were certain the businesses would reopen after temporarily closing after the various natural disasters. Also, P5 was certain of reopening based on cash on hand, good insurance, and a good insurance agent.

Participants believed the self–efficacy behavioral component of vested interest theory prevented the businesses from permanent failure in the aftermath of the disaster. P4 was certain after the fire that the business would reopen after temporarily relocating the business for 3–months after the disaster. P4 noted how self–efficacy and quick response prevented permanent business failure after the catastrophe. P5 described how rival firms and another business professional in the community who provided additional aid in the aftermath of the tornado enhanced the business owners' self–efficacy. P1, 2, 4 and 5 were certain of surviving the disaster experience. Self–confidence is essential to business survival.

Immediacy Effect of Natural Disasters

Participants also described how the VI theory immediacy behavioral component was an essential factor during the aftermath process. Pena, Zahran, Underwood, and Weiler (2014) noted the immediacy of generous donors' assistance prevented business failure in the aftermath of the disaster. P1 commented that friends, family, and cash reserves provided immediate support in the wake of Hurricane Matthew. P2 described starting repairs and restoration immediately after the natural disaster was over to prevent profit and customer loss. P1, 3, 4, and 5 described immediacy behaviors as the primary action during the aftermath of the disasters. Participants described themes found in the literature on small businesses surviving natural disasters.

Findings Related to the Natural Disaster Literature

The small business owners demonstrated successful business practice strategies related to the literature by avoiding permanent business closure in the aftermath of a natural disaster. Participants provided new lessons that small business owners could use to prevent demise from a natural disaster. Small business owners avoided or overcame the adverse effects of natural disasters and used several business strategies also found in the literature on natural disasters. Similar practices included (a) preparedness strategies, (b) recovery strategies, and (c) partnerships.

Preparedness strategies. Small business owners used a variety of strategies to prepare for natural disasters. Pathak and Ahmad (2016) suggested that investing in small business flood prevention would reduce the number of firms that fail in the aftermath of natural disasters. Many of the participants used sandbags to erect temporary barriers to prevent floodwaters. Sadiq and Graham (2015) noted the level of preparedness is not the same for every business because of its location. P3 preparedness strategy consisted of moving merchandise to another store location away from the disaster zone area. P2 strategy focused on the weather reports leading up to the natural disaster. Participants also noted using window shutters to prepare for the negative aftermath effects.

P4 described how management asked all employees for contact information in case of disaster emergency. Lamanna et al. (2012) suggested strategies that encompassed business closure, employees, and lifelines. Salman Sawalha (2014) noted that leaders of successful businesses focus on early warning strategies before, business continuity during, and damage assessment after disasters. Participants also worked with local disaster agencies to develop a strategic business disaster plan. Contrastingly, some participants did not have a written preparedness plan. Another strategy participants noted was the use of window shutters as a preparedness strategy.

Recovery strategies. Recovery strategies consisted of disaster planning reserve cash, insurance and friends and family assistance. Kahan (2015) noted that business disaster recovery plans should focus on the individual business operational needs. P4 recovery strategy included cash savings and insurance coverage. In contrast, Clay et al. (2016) noted that small business owners should focus on building social bonds to assist in recovery efforts. P3 acknowledged the business survived a natural disaster without flood insurance, but noted the business would have flood insurance for future catastrophes.

Partnerships. Participants noted partnerships with outreach organizations such as a local disaster preparedness agencies assisted with temporary employee housing and other acute necessities. Small business owners develop partnerships with private lending entities in the aftermath of natural disasters as a strategy to prevent permanent closure and expedite recovery (Franks & Johns, 2015). P3 used partnerships fostered with local municipalities to coordinate reconnection times of utility services after Hurricane Matthew. Franks and Johns (2015) suggested that library staff can help small business owners find suitable natural disaster partners in a community. The use of planned behavior and VI as systems thinking may be an innovative alternative to small business disaster preparedness.

Also, participants pointed out that the (SBA) set up temporary offices to help with disaster loan applications. Likewise, (FEMA) established temporary office sites to help with emergency loans and temporary housing. Participants also noted that local churches and other outreach groups provided human capital and financial support.

Applications to Professional Practice

Small business owners might apply the findings from this study as successful professional practices. Participants contributed to professional business practices related to the literature on the survival of small businesses in northeast Florida after a natural disaster. The secondary research on successful small businesses in northeast Florida was lacking. The lessons learned provided by the participants on strategies to survive the aftermath of natural disasters may enhance business researchers' ability to access related references. Business professionals can apply the findings from this study to improve their practices through (a) individual business readiness, (b) avoiding permanent business closure, and (c) additional survival factors and behaviors.

Business Readiness

Small business disaster readiness may avoid permanent closure after a catastrophe. Xiao and Peacock (2014) pointed out that since Hurricane Ike in 2008, small business owners have adopted mitigation efforts, and company leaders are more prepared for natural disasters. Some participants prepared with readiness plans that were either written or memorized. The natural disaster document analysis for P1 revealed a plan for wind damage, but the disaster plan did not have a flood plan. P' 2, 3, and 5 indicated that readiness plans were useful tools for surviving the aftermath of a natural disaster.

Many participants in northeast Florida concentrated on reopening after the natural disaster. P3 noted Florida experiences many natural disasters. Small business owners were happy to share lessons learned from surviving natural disasters in northeast Florida. The experience might increase mitigation efforts and change reactive behaviors to proactive intentions. Preventing small business closure in the aftermath of a catastrophe could reduce job loss and stimulate the economy.

P5 disaster plan did not include a plan for a natural disaster or fire, but it did include an employee contact list. Also, P5 initially planned for some types of natural disasters but did not plan for subsequent fires at the business as the result of the catastrophe. P4 and 5 did not have a plan but acknowledged that they would plan for future disasters.

Avoiding Permanent Business Closure

Florida is a coastal and inland area. Coastal areas are prone to natural disaster destruction (Morang, 2016). Inland areas are also prone, and destruction is just as severe (Priscoli & Stakhiv, 2015). Business owners may avoid permanent business closure by using power generators that provide a temporary power source. Small businesses may be without power for days or weeks after a natural catastrophe (Torres & Alsharif, 2016).

P1, 3, and 4 acquired power generators as a mitigation tool in the aftermath of natural disasters.

Business owners may research best practices including insurance coverage to avoid permanent business closure in northeastern Florida. Small business owners' costs without insurance and outside assistance surpass costs spent on government infrastructure (Patankar & Patwardhan, 2015). Best practices described P3 were controlling problems with utilities and building a disaster readiness network with business competitors.

Additional Survival Factors and Behaviors

Mancha and Yoder (2015) noted that TPB's intention–behavior was the most determinant factor in predicting disaster readiness. Participants who were proactive in their natural disaster preparation behaviors had less structural damage in the aftermath of a natural disaster. Taramelli, Valentini, and Sterlacchini (2015) noted that an example of natural disaster prevention behavior is retrofitting with shutters, improving roof structures, and installing a water–resistant barrier. P3 explained that the business owner primary behavioral focus should be reopening as soon as possible. P1 focused on reopening most of the businesses no later than 2 weeks after Hurricane Matthew. Participants looked at surviving in stages, including before, during, and after the natural disaster.

Some small business owners receive financial assistance from multiple donors (Marín, Bodin, Gelcich, & Crona, 2015). Donor funding from family and other sources assisted business owners in their efforts to remain open or to reopen quickly after the natural disaster. Coles, Zhang, and Zhuang (2016) noted small business owners' partnerships with donor organizations aided disaster recovery. Partnerships built by participants before the catastrophe contributed to business survival. Free assistance by family and friends after a natural disaster was immediate. Such aid did not require Internet access or legislative support. Participants also noted that private funders were eager to help prevent permanent business closure.

Participants frequently coordinated with public works departments after the catastrophe to maintain business operations. Small business owners' coordination with local government contradicts some of the data in the literature that focused just on governmental assistance and insurance premiums as critical success factors. The qualitative empirical evidence from business owners during the interview process indicated self–efficacy behaviors are essential factors in surviving natural disasters in northeastern Florida.

Implications for Social Change

Social change implications for small business owners include behaviorally preparing for natural disasters. Business owners who focus on proactive behaviors toward natural disasters prevent permanent business closure, unemployment, provide community stability, and economic growth. Also, business owners who avoid permanent business closure create an opportunity for increased market share as a result of demised companies that fail after a natural disaster.

The findings of this study may add to the body of knowledge and contribute to social change through the innovative family and friend coalitions that sustained established businesses after natural disasters. Asgary et al. (2012) contended that assistance from family and friends prevents permanent business closure in the aftermath of a natural disaster. Contrastingly, Lam, Arenas, Pace, LeSage, and Campanella, 2012 argued that federal assistance may predict small business recovery after a natural disaster. Business owners in this study created a conceptual framework that demonstrated best practices such as employing family and friends to help prepare for reopening immediately after the catastrophe. Shockley (2015) contended that social innovation might foster ideas for social change and solve challenging problems. Assistance from family, friends, and the business community produced the concept of disaster recovery through coalition building. This concept may prevent not only small businesses from failing in the aftermath of a natural disaster but also stimulate economic growth in the community.

Nongovernment organizations (NGOs) played a significant role in natural disaster survival of small businesses in northeast Florida. Also, Khan and Sayem (2013) contended that (NGOs) might be a key factor in recovery. Coles et al. (2016) noted (NGOs) are involved in disaster assistance and are policy advocates. Small business failure and employee displacement may affect community identity. The disaster recovery coalition concept of social change may also help sustain displaced families of employees whose businesses were affected by a natural catastrophe. Business owners' behavior changes through proactive disaster mitigation may provide opportunities for better communication with disaster readiness groups that may lead to better assistance for small businesses. Leaders who build partnerships increase the chances of their businesses surviving disasters and preventing other indirect damage.

Recommendations for Action

The qualitative multiple case study involved exploring strategies that business owners in northeastern Florida used to avoid permanent business closure in the aftermath of a natural disaster. Small business owners try to determine costs and possible damages when preparing for a natural disaster (Yang, Kajitani, Tatano & Jiang, 2016). Kajitani and Tatano (2014) suggested establishing a general estimate of loss from a natural disaster. Business leaders cannot afford to overlook flooding, especially in densely populated areas (Yang et al., 2016).

Recommendation 1: Construct Flood Barriers

I recommend small business owners construct flood barriers at the entrance and exit areas. Without using sandbags, inflatable bricks, and cement walls, participants believed floodwaters would have destroyed their businesses. I also recommend using inflatable foam as a barrier protection. Lessons learned led to using permanent or temporary flood barriers to protect property from flood damage. I further recommend concrete flooring with anti–mold micro padding.

Recommendation 2: Maintaining Adequate Insurance Coverage

I recommend maintaining adequate disaster insurance. Business owners' who did not have adequate insurance response after a catastrophe was often to purchase disaster insurance. I also recommend having an insurance agent who understands the individual business needs and provides adequate coverage including rebuilding costs for businesses in case of a catastrophe. I further recommend business preplan for disaster based on the business location and the possible unique hazards.

Recommendation 3: Damage and Destruction Aftermath

I recommend that small business owners keep cash reserves for damage and destruction in the aftermath of a natural disaster. Also, I recommend developing a network partnership with family, friends, and the community. I also recommend retrofitting company buildings that do not comply with local code. Working with local disaster agencies and retrofitting the business facility may increase qualifying for local, federal and international aid.

Recommendation 4: Learning from Experienced Business Owners

Lastly, I recommend learning from the lessons of business owners who have survived natural disasters. The recommendations from the research and findings may help (a) small business owners who do not have a natural disaster plan or would like to enhance the current plan, (b) new small business owners, and (c) community organizations. McKnight and Linnenluecke (2016) noted that businesses and community–based organization coalitions created sustainability and resilience. Such partnerships may reduce or prevent flooding and other natural–disaster–related business interruptions. Shepherd and Williams (2014) contended that community small–business-based coalitions have more compassion toward the effects of natural disasters. The findings of this study may increase the survival rate of small firms in northeastern Florida in the aftermath of natural disasters.

My goal is to distribute this study at conferences, training, and seminars in online and brick–and–mortar locations. I will provide all participants with a copy of the entire study, including results and findings. The study will also be ready for doctoral–research–based publication.

Recommendations for Further Study

Ajzen and Fishbein developed the theory of reasoned action in 1969 (Ajzen, 1985), Ajzen extended the theory of reasoned action in 1985 (Gagnon et al., 2015), and Crano developed VI theory (Crano, 1983). Adame and Miller (2016) noted that response and self–efficacy contributed to behavior related to surviving natural disasters. In contrast, Miller et al. (2013) suggested natural disaster preparedness behavior requires salience, certainty, and immediacy. In northeast Florida, small business owners may find it helpful to prepare for natural disasters because of the certainty and frequency of natural disasters.

The literature on the survival of small businesses in northeastern Florida after a natural disaster was limited. I recommend further qualitative research on natural disaster readiness among small businesses in North Florida compared to South Florida. I recommend further qualitative research on recent natural disasters using (TPB) and (VI) theory conceptual framework. More recent natural disaster studies may help refine the qualitative findings in this study. I also recommend conducting further research to explore the leadership attitudes, responses, and vested interest of small business owners. Business owners who focused on preparing for natural disasters through the use of disaster literature had a better chance surviving in the aftermath of a natural disaster.

Limitations Related to This Study

I limited the study to northeastern Florida, and the findings may not apply to other areas. I recommend conducting further research related to small business disaster preparedness behavior in northeastern Florida. I acknowledged that my former career as a public safety officer was a potential limitation. After conducting the interview process, I learned that experience in this field was an advantage. Being able to relate to the unique experiences of a natural disaster strike allowed participants to express themselves with greater detail.

A potential limitation of this study was the sample size. I also recommend conducting further research with more stakeholders. Another possible limitation may have been the number of interview questions. Participants seemed annoyed with the amount of time spent responding to the questions after the fifth interview question.

Reflections

My reflections on this study vary. During this journey, I discovered that perseverance and consistency generated progress regardless of the circumstances. I also learned that time management is a key to completing this program. The interview process gave me a better understanding of the attitudes and interest of business owners in preparing for the aftermath of a natural disaster. The high probability of natural disasters in Florida indicated the need for proactivity. I attempted to eliminate personal biases or any beliefs developed through my experiences as a first responder to natural disasters by following the interview protocol (see Appendix B), my consistent use of the interview protocol with every participant helped reduce any subconscious bias.

To add validity, I coded the keyword phrases participants used in the interview process. After a third party had transcribed the recorded interviews, I asked the participants to check their transcribed responses for accuracy. I ensured data saturation occurred after the interviews were complete so there would be no new information. Member checking increased the validity of the study.

My development as a researcher increased through interactions with the participants whose businesses survived natural disasters in northeastern Florida. The data collected from small business owners regarding their knowledge and experience greatly assisted with the findings. The participants seemed relieved to know that I had hands–on experience with natural disasters. The doctoral study process has made me a better critical thinker.

My ability to process information by breaking it down into parts has allowed me to make decisions based on facts and findings rather than perceptions and beliefs. I have relearned the importance of giving back to others. My doctoral committee guided me by responding and answering any questions I had related to the process of conducting the study and beyond.

Summary and Study Conclusions

Success strategies small business owners use to avoid permanent business closure in the aftermath of a natural disaster may also prevent job loss. These strategies may stabilize communities in the aftermath of natural disasters by creating and expanding business opportunities. Business owners in northeastern Florida may prevent business failure from natural disasters with a comprehensive natural disaster plan. Social change through natural disaster preparedness may also increase minority small business owners' chances of surviving the aftermath of a natural disaster.

There are many views on emergency planning. Some business leaders perceive planning to be a necessary tool for sustainability, whereas others are not convinced that planning makes a difference. The focus of this qualitative multiple case study was on business leaders who have successfully developed and implemented strategies that prevented business closure after a natural disaster. Positive attitudes are likely to benefit businesses when preparing for natural disasters. Business owner disaster mitigation may increase opportunities for better communication with all stakeholders. The owners of small firms that had plans in place demonstrated more positive responses in the wake of natural disasters compared to the owners of companies that did not have a plan in place. Participants also stated they had no doubt about reopening after the natural disaster, especially because their competitors came to their aid and wanted to see them succeed.

Business leaders can learn from the experiences described by others who have experienced natural disasters. Business leaders' intentions toward disaster planning may play a significant role in their decision making. The unexpected nature of disasters and their increased frequency may lead business leaders to develop emergency continuity planning as part of their business plan. Because natural disasters may cause small business failure, business leaders need preparedness and recovery plans to combat the possibly disastrous effects of natural disasters.

From a behavioral context, small businesses' success in the aftermath of natural disasters depends on business leaders' perceptions of natural disaster planning and the possible adverse effects these perceptions may have on business continuity. Small business owners may also benefit from learning about the difficulties that can potentially cause businesses to close permanently. Small business leaders in northeastern Florida as well as throughout the state of Florida and other coastal regions can take advantage of the lessons learned from other entrepreneurs who have developed effective strategies that enhance business continuity regarding disaster planning and recovery plans.

Appendix A: Tables

Table A1

10 Frequent Codes Mentioned by Participant

	P1	P2	P3	P4	P5	Frequency
Planning Experience	3	3	2	2	3	13
Insurance	1	2	3	0	3	9
Cash reserves and lifting merchandise of the floor	2	0	0	3	2	7
Recovery aftermath	3	3	0	3	3	12
Immediacy	3	3	2	3	3	14
Flood barriers	3	4	0	3	3	13
Protecting entrance and exit doors	2	4	0	2	2	12
Location	0	3	3	0	3	9
Family and friends	3	2	1	2	0	8

Table A2

Number of Sources by Category

Sources of literature	Number	Percent
Total Peer reviewed Sources	171	87.244%
Non-peer reviewed - Book	04	02.400%
Nonpeer reviewed - Journals	03	01.530%
Nonpeer reviewed – Other sources	04	02.400%
Total Nonpeer reviewed sources	11	05.612%
Total number of sources	196	

Table A3

Sources of Literature by Year

Time period	Number	Percent
2012 through 2016	182	90.62%
Before 2011	14	07.142%
Total # of sources	196	

Appendix B: Interview Protocols

Participants will e-mail a copy of the informed consent constituting their informed consent to participate as an unpaid and uncompensated volunteer in this study. The following statements provide the structure and procedure protocols for the interview:

1. I will begin by acknowledging that the participants have signed the consent form and ask if they have any questions about the study.

2. Ask the participant for permission to begin the audio recording of the interview.

3. If participant agrees to the audio recording, move on to Protocol 4.

4. Begin the audio recording.

5. Welcome each participant with these opening remarks: *"Hello, my name is Harry Kemp, and I am a Doctoral student at Walden University. Thank you so much for volunteering to participate in this study."*

6. *"The total time for this interview should be about 60 minutes."*

7. If the participant decides not to give their permission for an audio recording of the interview: *"Thank you (participant's name), I respect your decision. I need to take written notes of your responses to capture your perceptions about the mentoring program. The interview may require an additional time commitment to ensure I write your responses accurately. Are you still willing to participate?"*

8. Assure the participant that all responses will be confidential: *"(Participant's name) all of your responses are confidential, and the published doctoral study will not include any recognizing information to protect your identity."*

9. Check to make sure they received an email copy of the written informed consent form. Did you receive the document? The consent form includes the Walden Institutional Review Board (IRB) number for this study and an email address for the Chair of my Doctoral Study Committee. There is also an e-mail contact for the IRB if you have additional questions beyond this interview about the nature and purpose of this study.

10. *"Are you still willing to participate?"*

11. Explain the study's purpose and interview procedure: *"The purpose of this study is to understand the strategies you used help your business survive natural disasters."*

12. *"The interview format is open-ended questions. Please feel free to add clarifying remarks you deem appropriate."*

13. Statement of consent and option to withdraw from the interview process: *"(Participant's name) this interview is voluntary, and you may decline to answer any question that makes you feel uncomfortable. Additionally, you may withdraw your consent at any time, during this interview (given by you) and all notes, references, and recorded information previously collected enters a destruction process. Your withdrawal does not impose any reprisal or negatively affect your professional standing."*

14. Begin asking the interview questions.

15. After participant answers, all questions, "Thank you (participant's name) again for your willingness to participate in the study

16. Advise participant that they will receive a copy of the transcribed interpretation of

   the audio recording. (Participant's name), I will send you a copy of the

   transcribed notes from this audio recording. Once you receive the document,

   please review for accuracy, sign the document, and return it using (Walden e-mail

   address). Thank you again for your time and sharing your wisdom."

Appendix C: Interview Questions

I used the following interview questions in this qualitative case study. The focus of Question 1 is on the problem statement. Question 2 is the initial research question. Questions 4 and 5 relate to some important aspects of the small business natural disaster framework. Question 6 ensures the rich depth of the interview.

1. What is your experience with planning for a natural disaster?

2. How have you, as a business owner in northeast Florida, avoided permanent business closure in the aftermath of a natural disaster?

3. What strategies did your business implement during the natural disaster you experienced?

4. What were the business norms, attitudes, and responses immediately following the natural disaster?

5. How did self-efficacy (confidence) in your procedure help your business in the aftermath of a natural disaster?

6. How much damage and destruction has a natural disaster caused to your business?

7. Please elaborate on different strategies your business might enact to avoid permanent business closure from a natural disaster?

References

Abu-Qamar, M., & Wilson, A. (2012). The lived experience of a foot burn injury from the perspective of seven Jordanians with diabetes: A hermeneutic phenomenological study. *International Wound Journal, 9*, 33–43. doi:10.1111/j.1742-481X.2011.00837.x

Adame, B., & Miller, C. H. (2016). Vested interest: Developing scales for assessing flooding preparedness. *Disaster Prevention and Management: An International Journal, 25*, 282-297. doi:10.1108/dpm-08-2015-0196

Adame, B. J., & Miller, C. H. (2015). Vested interest, disaster preparedness, and strategic campaign message design. *Health Communication, 30*, 271–281. doi:10.1080/10410236.2013.842527

Ajzen, I. (1985). From intentions to actions: A theory of planned behavior. In J. Kuhl & J. Beckmann (Eds.), *Action control* (pp. 11–39). Berlin, Germany: Springer-Verlag.

Ajzen, I. (2005). *Attitudes, personality, and behavior.* Maidenhead, Berkshire, England: Open University Press.

Ajzen, I., Joyce, N., Sheikh, S., & Cote, N. G. (2011). Knowledge and the prediction of behavior: The role of information accuracy in the theory of planned behavior. *Basic and Applied Social Psychology, 33*, 101–117. doi:10.1080/01973533.2011.568834

Ajzen, I., & Klobas, J. (2013). Fertility intentions: An approach based on the theory of

planned behavior. *Demographic Research, 29*, 203–232.

doi:10.4054/DemRes.2013.29.8

Ajzen, I., & Sheikh, S. (2013). Action versus inaction: Anticipated affect in the theory of

planned behavior. *Journal of Applied Social Psychology, 43*, 155–162.

doi:10.1111/j.1559-1816.2012.00989.x

Akila, D. R. A., & Padmavathy, N. P. (2012). Capacity management and job scheduling

at Bogie Frame Shop in Integral Coach Factory–Chennai. *International Journal of

Scientific Research, 2*, 249-251. doi:10.15373/22778179/feb2013/83

Alipour, F., Khankeh, H., Fekrazad, H., Kamali, M., Rafiey, H., & Ahmadi, S. (2015).

Social issues and post-disaster recovery: A qualitative study in an Iranian context.

International Social Work, 58, 689-703. doi:10.1177/0020872815584426

Alló, M., & Loureiro, M. L. (2014). The role of social norms on preferences towards

climate change policies: A meta-analysis. *Energy Policy, 73,* 563–574.

doi:10.1016/j.enpol.2014.04.042

Altay, N., Prasad, S., & Tata, J. (2013). A dynamic model for costing disaster mitigation

policies. *Disasters, 37*, 357-373. doi:10.1111/disa.12004

Al-Yateem, N. (2012). The effect of interview recording on quality of data obtained: A

methodological reflection. *Nurse Researcher, 19*(4), 31–35. doi:10.7748/nr2012

.07.19.4.31.c9222

Anderson, C. A., Leahy, M. J., DelValle, R., Sherman, S., & Tansey, T. N. (2014).

Methodological application of multiple case study design using modified consensual qualitative research (CQR) analysis to identify best practices and

organizational factors in the public rehabilitation program. *Journal of Vocational*

Rehabilitation, 41(2), 87–98. doi:10.3233/JVR-140709

Archer, D. R., & Fowler, H. J. (2015). Characterising flash flood response to intense

rainfall and impacts using historical information and gauged data in Britain.

Journal of Flood Risk Management. Advance online publication.

doi:10.1111/jfr3.12187

Arendt, S. W., Roberts, K. R., Strohbehn, C., Ellis, J., Paez, P., & Meyer, J. (2012). Use

of qualitative research in foodservice organizations. *International Journal of*

Contemporary Hospitality Management, 24, 820–837.

doi:10.1108/09596111211247182

Arghode, V. (2012). Qualitative and quantitative research: Paradigmatic differences.

Global Education Journal, 4, 155–163. Retrieved from

http://www.franklinpublishing.net/globaleducation.html

Ariza, E., Lindeman, K. C., Mozumder, P., & Suman, D. O. (2014). Beach management

in Florida: Assessing stakeholder perceptions on governance. *Ocean And Coastal*

Management, 9682–93. doi:10.1016/j.ocecoaman.2014.04.033

Asgary, A., Anjum, M. I., & Azimi, N. (2012). Disaster recovery and business continuity

after the 2010 flood in Pakistan: Case of small businesses. *International Journal*

of Disaster Risk Reduction, 2, 46–56. doi:10.1016/j.ijdrr.2012.08.001

Atkinson, C. L., & Sapat, A. K. (2014). Hurricane Wilma and long–term business

recovery in disasters: The role of local government procurement and economic development. *Journal of Homeland Security & Emergency Management, 11*, 169–192. doi:10.1515/jhsem-2013-0002

Ayala, J.-C., & Manzano, G. (2014). The resilience of the entrepreneur. Influence on the success of the business: A longitudinal analysis. *Journal of Economic Psychology, 42*, 126–135. doi:10.1016/j.joep.2014.02.004

Baba, H., Watanabe, T., Nagaishi, M., & Matsumoto, H. (2014). Area business continuity management: A new opportunity for building economic resilience. *Procedia Economics and Finance, 18*, 296-303. doi:10.1016/s2212-5671(14)00943–5

Baker, C. R. (2014). Breakdowns of accountability in the face of natural disasters: The case of Hurricane Katrina. *Critical Perspectives on Accounting, 25*, 620–632. doi:10.1016/j.cpa.2014.02.005.

Bang, H. N. (2012). Disaster management in Cameroon: The Lake Nyos disaster experience. *Disaster Prevention & Management, 21*, 489–506. doi:10.1108/09653561211256189

Barnham, C. (2012). Separating methodologies. *International Journal of Market Research, 54,* 736-738. doi:10.2501/IJMR-54-6-736-738

Baruch, Y., Wordsworth, R., Mills, C., & Wright, S. (2015). Career and work attitudes of blue-collar workers, and the impact of a natural disaster chance event on the relationships between intention to quit and actual quit behaviour. *European Journal of Work and Organizational Psychology, 25*, 459–473. doi:10.1080/1359432x.2015.1113168

Baškarada, S. (2014). Qualitative case study guidelines. *Qualitative Report, 19*(40), 1–15.

Retrieved from http://tqr.nova.edu/

Bayer, A. D., Pugh, T. A., Krause, A., & Arneth, A. (2015). Historical and future

quantification of terrestrial carbon sequestration from a Greenhouse–gas–value

perspective. *Global Environmental Change, 32,* 153–164. doi:10.1016/j

.gloenvcha.2015.03.004

Bellone, J. J., Navarick, D. J., & Mendoza, R. (2012). Participant withdrawal as a

function of hedonic value of task and time of semester. *Psychological Record, 62,*

395–407. Retrieved from

http://thepsychologicalrecord.siu.edu/Summer_2012.html

Benoot, C., Hannes, K., & Bilsen, J. (2016). The use of purposeful sampling in a

qualitative evidence synthesis: A worked example on sexual adjustment to a

cancer trajectory. *BMC Medical Research Methodology, 16*. doi:10.1186/s12874-

016-0114-6

Berke, P., Cooper, J., Aminto, M., Grabich, S., & Horney, J. (2014). Adaptive planning

for disaster recovery and resiliency: An evaluation of 87 local recovery plans in

eight states. *Journal of the American Planning Association, 80*, 310–323.

doi:10.1080/01944363.2014.976585

Bernard, E., & Titov, V. (2015). Evolution of tsunami warning systems and products.

Philosophical Transactions of the Royal Society A: Mathematical, Physical and

Engineering Sciences, 373(2053), 20140371. doi:10.1098/rsta.2014.0371

Bevan, M. T. (2014). A method of phenomenological interviewing. *Qualitative Health Research, 24*, 136–144. doi:10.1177/1049732313519710

Bezzina, F., & Saunders, M. (2014). The pervasiveness and implications of statistical misconceptions among academics with a special interest in business research methods. *Electronic Journal of Business Research Methods, 12*(2), 29–40. Retrieved from http://www.ejbrm.com

Blake, E. S., Landsea, C., & Gibney, E. J. (2007). The deadliest, costliest, and most intense United States tropical cyclones from 1851 to 2006 (and other frequently requested hurricane facts). Retrieved from http://www.srh.noaa.gov/www/images /tbw/1921/DeadliestHurricanes.pdf

Bledsoe, M. J., & Grizzle, W. E. (2013). Ethical issues in tissue research: Use of human specimens in research: The evolving United States regulatory, policy, and scientific landscape. *Diagnostic Histopathology, 19*, 322–330. doi:10.1016/j.mpdhp.2013.06.015

Blöschl, G., Gaál, L., Hall, J., Kiss, A., Komma, J., Nester, T., & Viglione, A. (2015). Increasing river floods: Fiction or reality? *Wiley Interdisciplinary Reviews: Water, 2*, 329–344. doi:10.1002/wat2.1079

Boblin, S. L., Ireland, S., Kirkpatrick, H., & Robertson, K. (2013). Using Stake's qualitative case study approach to explore implementation of evidence–based practice. *Qualitative Health Research, 23*, 1267–1275. doi:10.1177/1049732313502128

Borrego, M., Foster, M. J., & Froyd, J. E. (2014). Systematic literature reviews in

engineering education and other developing interdisciplinary fields. *Journal of*

Engineering Education, 103, 45–76. doi:10.1002/jee.20038

Boustan, L. P., Kahn, M. E., & Rhode, P. W. (2012). Moving to higher ground:

Migration response to natural disasters in the early twentieth century. *American*

Economic Review, 102, 238–244. doi:10.1257/aer.102.3.238

Bowen, K. J., & Friel, S. (2012). Climate change adaptation: Where does global health fit

in the agenda? *Global Health, 8*, 10. doi:10.1186/1744–8603-8-10

Bullough, A., Renko, M., & Myatt, T. (2014). Danger zone entrepreneurs: The

importance of resilience and self-efficacy for entrepreneurial intentions.

entrepreneurship. *Theory & Practice, 38*, 473–499. doi:10.1111/etap.12006

Bulpitt, H., & Martin, P. J. (2010). Who am I and what am I doing? Becoming a

qualitative research interviewer. *Nurse Researcher, 17*(3), 7–16.

doi:10.7748/nr2010.04.17.3.7.c7741

Cameron, L., & Shah, M. (2015). Risk-taking behavior in the wake of natural disasters.

Journal of Human Resources, 50, 484–515. doi:10.3368/jhr.50.2.484

Campbell, V. (2014). Framing environmental risks and natural disasters in factual

entertainment television. *Environmental Communication, 8*(1), 58–74.

doi:10.1080/17524032.2013.848222

Carter, N., Bryant-Lukosius, D., DiCenso, A., Blythe, J., & Neville, A. J. (2014). The use

of triangulation in qualitative research. *Oncology Nursing Forum, 41*(5).

Retrieved from http://www.ons.org/

Cartwright, J. C., Hickman, S. E., Nelson, C. A., & Knafl, K. A. (2013). Investigators'
successful strategies for working with institutional review boards. *Research in
Nursing & Health, 36*, 478–486. doi:10.1002/nur.21553

Chamlee-Wright, E., & Storr, V. H. (2014). Commercial relationships and spaces after
disaster. *Society, 51*, 656–664. doi:10.1007/s12115–014–9849-z

Chatterjee, C., & Mozumder, P. (2015). Hurricane Wilma, utility disruption, and
household wellbeing. *International Journal of Disaster Risk Reduction, 14*, 395–
402. doi:10.1016/j.ijdrr.2015.09.005

Chen, M. (2016). Extending the theory of planned behavior model to explain people's
energy savings and carbon reduction behavioral intentions to mitigate climate
change in Taiwan–Moral obligation matters. *Journal of Cleaner Production, 112*,
1746–1753. doi:10.1016/j.jclepro.2015.07.043

Chenoweth, M., & Mock, C. J. (2013). Hurricane "Amanda": Rediscovery of a forgotten
U.S. Civil War Florida hurricane. *Bulletin of the American Meteorological
Society, 94*, 1735–1742. doi:10.1175/bams-d-12-00171.1

Chien, G. C. L., Yen, I.-Y., & Hoang, P.-Q. (2012). Combination of theory of planned
behavior and motivation: An exploratory study of potential beach–based resorts in
Vietnam. *Asia Pacific Journal of Tourism Research, 17*, 489–508.
doi:10.1080/10941665.2011.627352

Chikoto, G. L., Sadiq, A., & Fordyce, E. (2013). Disaster mitigation and preparedness:
Comparison of nonprofit, public, and private organizations. *Nonprofit &
Voluntary Sector Quarterly, 42*, 391–410. doi:10.1177/0899764012452042

Chinh, D. T., Bubeck, P., Dung, N. V., & Kreibich, H. (2016). The 2011 flood event in

the Mekong Delta: preparedness, response, damage and recovery of private

households and small businesses. *Disasters, 40*, 753–778. doi:10.1111/disa.12171

Choi, J. N. (2012). Context and creativity: The theory of planned behavior as an

alternative mechanism. *Social Behavior Personal, 40*, 681–692.

doi:10.2224/sbp.2012.40.4.681

Clarke, D. J., & Grenham, D. (2013). Microinsurance and natural disasters: Challenges

and options. *Environmental Science and Policy, 27*, S89-S98.

doi:10.1016/j.envsci.2012.06.005

Clay, P. M., Colburn, L. L., & Seara, T. (2016). Social bonds and recovery: An analysis

of Hurricane Sandy in the first year after landfall. *Marine Policy*,

doi:10.1016/j.marpol.2016.04.049

Colbert, P., Wyatt-Smith, C., & Klenowski, V. (2012). A systems–level approach to

building sustainable assessment cultures: Moderation, quality task design and

dependability of judgement. *Policy Futures in Education, 10*, 386–401.

doi:10.2304/pfie.2012.10.4.386

Coles, J., Zhang, J., & Zhuang, J. (2016). Partnership behavior in disaster relief

operations: a case study comparison of the responses to the tornado in Joplin,

Missouri and Hurricane Sandy along the Jersey Coast. *Natural Hazards, 84*, 625–

647. doi:10.1007/s11069–016–2445–3

Collier, S. J., & Lakoff, A. (2014). Vital systems security: Reflexive biopolitics and the government of emergency. *Theory, Culture & Society, 32*(2), 19–51. doi:10.1177/0263276413510050

Cox, T. (2012). Community resilience and decision theory challenges for catastrophic events. *Risk Analysis, 32*, 1919–1934. doi:10.1111/j.1539-6924.2012.01881.x

Crano, W. D. (1983). Assumed consensus of attitudes: The effect of vested interest. *Personality and Social Psychology Bulletin, 9*, 597–608. doi:10.1177/0146167283094009

Crano, W., & Prislin, R. (1995). Components of vested interest and attitude–behavior consistency. *Basic & Applied Social Psychology, 17*(1), 1–21. doi:10.1207/s15324834basp1701&2_1

Cunado, J., & Ferreira, S. (2013). The macroeconomic impacts of natural disasters: The case of floods. *Land Economics, 90*, 149–168. doi:10.3368/le.90.1.149

Dar, O., Buckley, E. J., Rokadiya, S., Huda, Q., & Abrahams, J. (2014). Integrating health into disaster risk reduction strategies: Key considerations for success. *American Journal of Public Health, 104*, 1811-1816. doi:10.2105/ajph.2014.302134

Daramola, A. Y., Oni, O. T., Ogundele, O., & Adesanya, A. (2016). Adaptive capacity and coping response strategies to natural disasters: A study in Nigeria. *International Journal of Disaster Risk Reduction, 15*, 132–147. doi:10.1016/j.ijdrr.2016.01.007

Dasgupta, M. (2015). Exploring the relevance of case study research. *Vision: The Journal of Business Perspective, 19*, 147–160. doi:10.1177/0972262915575661

Davies, G. (2014). The emergence of a national politics of disaster, 1865–1900. *Journal of Policy History, 26*, 305–326. doi:10.1017/S0898030614000141

De Dominicis, S., Crano, W. D., Ganucci Cancellieri, U., Mosco, B., Bonnes, M., Hohman, Z., & Bonaiuto, M. (2014). Vested interest and environmental risk communication: Improving willingness to cope with impending disasters. *Journal of Applied Social Psychology, 44*, 364–374. doi:10.1111/jasp.12229

De Mel, S., McKenzie, D., & Woodruff, C. (2012). Enterprise recovery following natural disasters. *Economic Journal, 122*(559), 64–91. doi:10.1111/j.1468-0297.2011.02475.x

Denzin, N. K., & Lincoln, Y. S. (2011). *The Sage handbook of qualitative research* (4th ed.). Thousand Oaks, CA: Sage.

De Souza, S. V., Yukio, K., & Dollery, B. (2015). Post–disaster local infrastructure reconstruction finance: A comparative analysis of policy intervention in the Japanese earthquake and Queensland flood disasters. *Public Finance & Management, 15*, 65. Retrieved from http://www.spaef.com/pfm.php

Doody, O., & Doody, C. M. (2015). Conducting a pilot study: Case study of a novice researcher. *British Journal of Nursing, 24*, 1074-1078. doi:10.12968/bjon.2015.24.21.1074

Doern, R. (2016). Entrepreneurship and crisis management: The experiences of small businesses during the London 2011 riots. *International Small Business Journal, 34*, 276–302. doi:10.1177/0266242614553863

Doykos, B., Brinkley-Rubinstein, L., Craven, K., McCormack, M., & Geller, J. (2014). Leveraging identity, gaining access: Explorations of self in diverse field–based research settings. *Journal of Community Practice, 22*, 130–149. doi:10.1080/10705422.2014.901265

Dufty, N. (2012). Using social media to build community disaster resilience. *Australian Journal of Emergency Management, 27*, 40. Retrieved from http://www.em.gov.au/Publications/Australianjournalofemergencymanagement/Pages/default.aspx

Dulière, V., Zhang, Y., & Salathé, E. P. (2013). Changes in twentieth-century extreme temperature and precipitation over the Western United States based on observations and regional climate model simulations. *Journal of Climate, 26*, 8556–8575. doi:10.1175/JCLI-D-12-00818.1

Dyl, J. (2009). Lessons from history: Coastal cities and natural disaster. *Management of Environmental Quality: An International Journal, 20*, 460–473. doi:10.1108/14777830910963780

Eiser, J. R., Bostrom, A., Burton, I., Johnston, D. M., McClure, J., Paton, D., & White, M. P. (2012). Risk interpretation and action: A conceptual framework for responses to natural hazards. *International Journal of Disaster Risk Reduction, 1*, 5–16. doi:10.1016/j.ijdrr.2012.05.002

Ejeta, L. T., Ardalan, A., & Paton, D. (2015). Application of behavioral theories to

disaster and emergency health preparedness: A systematic review. *PLoS Currents,*

7. doi:10.1371/10.1371/currents.dis.31a8995ced321301466db400f1357829

Emerson, R. W. (2015). Convenience sampling, random sampling, and snowball

sampling: How does sampling affect the validity of research? *Journal of Visual*

Impairment & Blindness, 109, 164-168. Retrieved from http://www.afb.org

Englander, M. (2012). The interview: Data collection in descriptive phenomenological

human scientific research. *Journal of Phenomenological Psychology, 43*, 13–35.

doi:10.1163/156916212X632943

Epstein, B., & Khan, D. C. (2014). Application impact analysis: A risk-based approach to

business continuity and disaster recovery. *Journal of Business Continuity &*

Emergency Planning, 7, 230–237. Retrieved from

http://www.henrystewartpublications.com/jbcep

Ewing, B. T., Kruse, J. B., & Thompson, M. A. (2005). Empirical examination of the

Corpus Christi unemployment rate and Hurricane Bret. *Natural Hazards Review,*

6(4), 191–196. doi:10.1061/(ASCE)1527-6988(2005)6:4(191)

Farazmand, A. (2014). *Crisis and emergency management: Theory and practice.* Boca

Raton, FL: Taylor and Francis

Farrelly, P. (2013). Choosing the right method for a quantitative study. *British Journal of*

School Nursing, 8, 42–44. doi:10.12968/bjsn.2013.8.1.42

Fassinger, R., & Morrow, S. (2013). Toward best practices in quantitative, qualitative,

and mixed–method research: A social justice perspective. *Journal for Social*

Action in Counseling and Psychology, 5(2), 69–83. Retrieved from

http://www.psysr.org/jsacp/

Federal Emergency Management Agency. (2015a). *Effective coordination of recovery*

resources for state, tribal, territorial and local incidents. Retrieved from

http://www.fema.gov/media-library-data/1423604728233-

1d76a43cabf1209678054c0828bbe8b8/EffectiveCoordinationofRecoveryResourc

esGuide020515vFNL.pdf

Federal Emergency Management Agency. (2015b). *Protecting your businesses.* Retrieved

from http://www.fema.gov/protecting–your–businesses

Filatova, T. (2014). Market–based instruments for flood risk management: A review of

theory, practice and perspectives for climate adaptation policy. *Environmental*

Science & Policy, 37, 227–242. doi:10.1016/j.envsci.2013.09.005

Fischer-Smith, R. (2013). The Earthquake Support Subsidy for Christchurch's small and

medium enterprises: Perspectives from business owners. *Small Enterprise*

Research, 20, 40–54. doi:10.5172/ser.2013.20.1.40

Franks, J. E., & Johns, C. (2015). Entrepreneur assistance & economic development in

Florida libraries. *Reference Services Review, 43*, 400–418. doi:10.1108/rsr–03–

2015–0014

Frechtling, D., & Boo, S. (2012). On the ethics of management research: An exploratory

investigation. *Journal of Business Ethics, 106*, 149–160. doi:10.1007/s10551–

011–0986–7

Friedland, K. D., & Hare, J. A. (2007). Long–term trends and regime shifts in sea surface

temperature on the continental shelf of the northeast United States. *Continental

Shelf Research, 27*, 2313–2328. doi:10.1016/j.csr.2007.06.001

Fuhrmann, C. M., Konrad, C. E., Kovach, M. M., McLeod, J. T., Schmitz, W. G., &

Dixon, P. G. (2014). Ranking of tornado outbreaks across the United States and

their climatological characteristics. *Weather and Forecasting, 29*, 684–701.

doi:10.1175/waf-d-1300128.1

Fusch, P. I., & Ness, L. R. (2015). Are we there yet? Data saturation in qualitative

research. *Qualitative Report, 20,* 1408–1416. Retrieved from http://tqr.nova.edu/

Gagnon, M., Cassista, J., Payne-Gagnon, J., & Martel, B. (2015). Applying the theory of

planned behaviour to understand nurse intention to follow recommendations

related to a preventive clinical practice. *Journal of Research in Nursing, 20*, 582–

593. doi:10.1177/1744987115611715

Galeotti, M., Gürtler, M., & Winkelvos, C. (2012). Accuracy of premium calculation

models for CAT bonds: An empirical analysis. *Journal of Risk and Insurance, 80*,

401–421. doi:10.1111/j.1539-6975.2012.01482.x

Gin, J. L., Kranke, D., Saia, R., & Dobalian, A. (2016). Disaster preparedness in

homeless residential organizations in Los Angeles County: Identifying needs,

assessing gaps. *National Hazards Review, 17*. doi:10.1061/(asce)nh.1527-

6996.0000208

Giorgi, A. (2012). The descriptive phenomenological psychological method. *Journal of

Phenomenological Psychology, 43*, 3–12. doi:10.1163/156916212x632934

Goshay, R. C., Dacy, D. C., & Kunreuther, H. (1970). The economics of natural

disasters: Implications for federal policy. *Journal of Risk and Insurance, 37*, 664–

668. doi:10.2307/251080

Gotham, K. F. (2013). Dilemmas of disaster zones: Tax incentives and business

reinvestment in the Gulf Coast after Hurricanes Katrina and Rita. *City &*

Community, 12, 291–308. doi:10.1111/cico.12048

Greaney, A., Sheehy, A., Heffernan, C., Murphy, J., Mhaolrúnaigh, S. N., Heffernan, E.,

& Brown, G. (2012). Research ethics application: A guide for the novice

researcher. *British Journal of Nursing, 21*, 38–43. Retrieved from

http://www.markallengroup.com/ma-healthcare

Guo, Y., & Li, Y. (2016). Getting ready for mega disasters: The role of past experience in

changing disaster consciousness. *Disaster Prevention and Management: An*

International Journal, 25, 492–505. doi:10.1108/dpm-01-2016-0008

Guster, D. C., Lee, O. F., & McCann, B. P. (2012). Outsourcing and replication

considerations in disaster recovery planning. *Disaster Prevention and*

Management, 21, 172–183. doi:10.1108/09653561211219982

Guy, R., & Lownes-Jackson, M. (2011). Business continuity strategies: An assessment of

planning, preparedness, response and recovery activities for emergency disasters.

Review of Management Innovation & Creativity, 4(9), 55–69. Retrieved from

http://www.intellectbase.org/journals.php#RMIC

Hamdan, F. (2015). Intensive and extensive disaster risk drivers and interactions with

recent trends in the global political economy, with special emphasis on rentier states. *International Journal of Disaster Risk Reduction, 14*, 273–289.

doi:10.1016/j.ijdrr.2014.09.004

Hayakawa, K., Matsuura, T., & Okubo, F. (2015). Firm-level impacts of natural disasters

on production networks: Evidence from a flood in Thailand. *Journal of the*

Japanese and International Economies, 38, 244–259.

doi:10.1016/j.jjie.2015.10.001

Hayashi, M. (2012). A quick method for assessing economic damage caused by natural

disasters: An epidemiological approach. *International Advances in Economic*

Research, 18, 417–427. doi:10.1007/s11294-012-9367-y

Heale, R., & Forbes, D. (2013). Understanding triangulation in research. *Evidence–Based*

Nursing, 16, 98. doi:10.1136/eb–2013-101494

Hémond, Y., & Benoît, R. (2012). Preparedness: The state of the art and future prospects.

Disaster Prevention and Management, 21, 404–417.

doi:10.1108/09653561211256125

Herbane, B. (2010). The evolution of business continuity management: A historical

review of practices and drivers. *Business History, 52*, 978–1002.

doi:10.1080/00076791.2010.511185

Herbane, B. (2013). Exploring crisis management in UK small- and medium-sized

enterprises. *Journal of Contingencies & Crisis Management, 21*(2), 82–95.

doi:10.1111/1468–5973.12006

Hernantes, J., Rich, E., Laugé, A., Labaka, L., & Sarriegi, J. M. (2013). Learning before

the storm: Modeling multiple stakeholder activities in support of crisis management, a practical case. *Technological Forecasting & Social Change, 80,* 1742–1755. doi:10.1016/j.techfore.2013.01.002

Hirano, J., Kishi, K., Narupiti, S., Choocharukul, K., & Nakatsuji, T. (2014). Influence of daily SNS usage on the collection of disaster information and people's behavior during a flood. *Asian Transport Studies, 3,* 171–186. doi:10.11175/eastsats.3.171

Holloway, I., & Wheeler, S. (2013). *Qualitative research in nursing and healthcare.* Chicester, England: Wiley-Blackwell.

Hoong, L. L., & Marthandan, G. (2014). Critical dimensions of disaster recovery planning. *International Journal of Business and Management, 9*(12), 145–158. doi:10.5539/ijbm.v9n12p145

Hopkins, D. (2014). The sustainability of climate change adaptation strategies in New Zealand's ski industry: A range of stakeholder perceptions. *Journal of Sustainable Tourism, 22,* 107–126. doi:10.1080/09669582.2013.804830

Houghton, C., Casey, D., Shaw, D., & Murphy, K. (2013). Rigour in qualitative case-study research. *Nurse Researcher, 20*(4), 12–17. doi:10.7748/nr2013.03.20.4.12.e326

Houston, J. B., Pfefferbaum, B., & Rosenholtz, C. E. (2012). Disaster news: Framing and frame changing in coverage of major U.S. natural disasters, 2000–2010. *Journalism & Mass Communication Quarterly, 89,* 606–623. doi:10.1177/1077699012456022

Howat, H., Curtis, N., Landry, S., Farmer, K., Kroll, T., & Douglass, J. (2012). Lessons from crisis recovery in schools: how hurricanes impacted schools, families and the community. *School Leadership & Management, 32*, 487–501.

doi:10.1080/13632434.2012.723613

Howe, P. D., Boudet, H., Leiserowitz, A., & Maibach, E. W. (2014). Mapping the

shadow of experience of extreme weather events. *Climatic Change, 127*, 381–

389. doi:10.1007/s10584-014-1253-6

Husby, T. G., de Groot, H. L., Hofkes, M. W., & Dröes, M. I. (2014). Do floods have

permanent effects? Evidence from the Netherlands. *Journal of Regional Science,

54*, 355–377. doi:10.1111/jors.12112

Ikse, S. D., & Lengfellner, L. G. (2015). Fire, water and books: Disaster preparedness for

academic libraries. *Professional Safety, 60*(10), 39–46. Retrieved from

http://www.asse.org/bprofe1.htm

Ingirige, B., & Wedawatta, G. (2014). Putting policy initiatives into practice. *Structural

Survey, 32*, 123-139. doi:10.1108/ss-01-2013-0011

Ivey, J. (2015). Demystifying research. How important is a conceptual framework?

Pediatric Nursing, 41(3), 145–153. Retrieved from

http://www.ajj.com/services/pblshng/pnj/default.htm

Izumi, T., & Shaw, R. (2014). A new approach of disaster management in Bangladesh:

Private sector involvement. *Risk, Hazards & Crisis in Public Policy, 5*, 425.

doi:10.1002/rhc3.12069

Johnson, B. D., Dunlap, E., & Benoit, E. (2010). Organizing "mountains of words" for

data analysis, both qualitative and quantitative. *Substance Use & Misuse, 45*,

648–670. doi:10.3109/10826081003594757

Johnson, I. M., Siegel, J. T., & Crano, W. D. (2014). Expanding the reach of vested

interest in predicting attitude–consistent behavior. *Social Influence, 9*, 20–36.

doi:10.1080/15534510.2012.738243

Johnson, L. A., & Hayashi, H. (2012). Synthesis efforts in disaster recovery research.

International Journal of Mass Emergencies & Disasters, 30, 212–239. Retrieved

from http://www.ijmed.org

Johnson, P., Buehring, A., Cassell, C., & Symon, G. (2007). Defining qualitative

management research: An empirical investigation. *Qualitative Research in

Organizations and Management: An International Journal, 2*, 23–42.

doi:10.1108/17465640710749108

Kahan, J. H. (2015). Hedging against terrorism: Are US businesses prepared? *Journal of

Business Continuity & Emergency Planning, 9*, 70–83. Retrieved from

http://www.henrystewartpublications.com/jbcep

Kajitani, Y., & Tatano, H. (2014). Estimation of production capacity loss rate after the

great east Japan earthquake and tsunami in 2011. *Economic Systems Research, 26*,

13–38. doi:10.1080/09535314.2013.872081

Kantur, D., & İşeri-Say, A. (2015). Measuring organizational resilience: A scale

development. *Journal of Business, Economics & Finance, 4*, 456–472.

doi:10.17261/Pressacademia.2015313066

Kaushalya, H., Karunasena, G., & Amarathunga, D. (2014). Role of insurance in post

disaster recovery planning in business community. *Procedia Economics and

Finance, 18*, 626–634. doi:10.1016/s2212-5671(14)00984-8

Kellens, W., Terpstra, T., & De Maeyer, P. (2012). Perception and communication of

flood risks: A systematic review of empirical research. *Risk Analysis, 33*, 24–49.

doi:10.1111/j.1539-6924.2012.01844.x

Kennedy-Clark, S. (2013). Research by design: Design-based research and the higher

degree research student. *Journal of Learning Design, 6*(2), 26–32.

doi:10.5204/jld.v6i2.128

Khan, M. A. U., & Sayem, M. A. (2013). Understanding recovery of small enterprises

from natural disaster. *Environmental Hazards, 12*, 218–239.

doi:10.1080/17477891.2012.761593

Kim, E., Ham, S., Yang, I. S., & Choi, J. G. (2013). The roles of attitude, subjective

norm, and perceived behavioral control in the formation of consumers' behavioral

intentions to read menu labels in the restaurant industry. *International Journal of

Hospitality Management, 35,* 203–213. doi:10.1016/j.ijhm.2013.06.008

Kirkwood, A., & Price, L. (2013). Examining some assumptions and limitations of

research on the effects of emerging technologies for teaching and learning in

higher education. *British Journal of Educational Technology, 44,* 536–543.

doi:10.1111/bjet.12049

Knight-Agarwal, C. R., Williams, L. T., Davis, D., Davey, R., Shepherd, R., Downing,

A., & Lawson, K. (2015). The perspectives of obese women receiving antenatal

care: A qualitative study of women's experiences. *Women and Birth.* Advance

online publication. doi:10.1016/j.wombi.2015.10.008

Knowles, S. G., & Kunreuther, H. C. (2014). Troubled Waters: The National Flood

Insurance Program in Historical Perspective. *Journal Of Policy History, 26*(3),

327–353. doi:10.1017/S0898030614000153

Kousky, C. (2014). Informing climate adaptation: A review of the economic costs of

natural disasters. *Energy Economics, 46*, 576–592. doi:10.1016/j.eneco.2013.09

.029

Kunreuther, H., Michel-Kerjan, E., & Pauly, M. (2013). Making America more resilient

toward natural disasters: A call for action. *Environment: Science and Policy for

Sustainable Development, 55*(4), 15–23. doi:10.1080/00139157.2013.803884

Kunreuther, H., & Michel-Kerjan, E. (2015). Demand for fixed-price multi-year

contracts: Experimental evidence from insurance decisions. *Journal of Risk

Uncertain, 51*(2), 171–194. doi:10.1007/s11166-015-9225-4

Kunreuther, H., & Weber, E. (2014). Aiding decision making to reduce the impacts of

climate change. *Journal of Consumer Policy, 37*, 397–411. doi:10.1007/s10603-

013-9251-z

Kunz, N., Reiner, G., & Gold, S. (2014). Investing in disaster management capabilities

versus pre-positioning inventory: A new approach to disaster preparedness.

International Journal of Production Economics, 157, 261–272.

doi:10.1016/j.ijpe.2013.11.002

Kusumasari, B., & Alam, Q. (2012). Local wisdom-based disaster recovery model in

Indonesia. *Disaster Prevention and Management, 21*, 351–369.

doi:10.1108/09653561211234525

Lam, N. S. N., Arenas, H., Pace, K., LeSage, J., & Campanella, R. (2012). Predictors of

business return in New Orleans after Hurricane Katrina. *PLoS ONE, 7*(10),

e47935. doi:10.1371/journal.pone.0047935

Lamanna, Z., Williams, K. H., & Childers, C. (2012). An assessment of resilience:

Disaster management and recovery for greater New Orleans' hotels. *Journal of

Human Resources in Hospitality & Tourism, 11*, 210–224.

doi:10.1080/15332845.2012.668653

Landrum, B., & Garza, G. (2015). Mending fences: Defining the domains and approaches

of quantitative and qualitative research. *Qualitative Psychology, 2*, 199–209.

doi:10.1037/qup0000030

Latha, B., Gowsalya, B., & Kannega, 2014. Procuring the Dropbox using honey

encryption technique. *Applied Mechanics and Materials, 573*, 523–528.

doi:10.4028/www.scientific.net/AMM.573.523

Lazzaroni, S., & van Bergeijk, P. A. (2014). Natural disasters' impact, factors of

resilience and development: A meta-analysis of the macroeconomic literature.

Ecological Economics, 10 (7) 333–346. doi:10.1016/j.ecolecon.2014.08.015

Leedy, P. D., & Ormrod, J. E. (2013). *Practical research: Planning and design.* Boston,

MA: Pearson.

Lei, Y., & Wang, J. (2014). A preliminary discussion on the opportunities and challenges

of linking climate change adaptation with disaster risk reduction. *Natural

Hazards, 71*, 1587–1597. doi:10.1007/s11069-013-0966-6

Levy, J., Yu, P., & Prizzia, R. (2016, May 24–27). *Business continuity planning for economic resilience in Hawaii.* Paper presented at the Global Conference on Business & Finance, San Jose, Costa Rica. Retrieved from http://www.theibfr.com/proceedings.htm

Lin, C., Siebeneck, L., Lindell, M., Prater, C., Wu, H., & Huang, S. (2014). Evacuees' information sources and reentry decision making in the aftermath of Hurricane Ike. *Natural Hazards, 70*, 865–882. doi:10.1007/s11069-013-0853-1

Lindell, M. K., & Perry, R. W. (2012). The protective action decision model: Theoretical modifications and additional evidence. *Risk Analysis, 32*, 616–632. doi:10.1111/j.1539-6924.2011.01647.x

Lindström, J. (2012). A model to explain a business contingency process. *Disaster Prevention and Management, 21*, 269–281. doi:10.1108/09653561211220052

Linnerooth–Bayer, J., & Hochrainer–Stigler, S. (2015). Financial instruments for disaster risk management and climate change adaptation. *Climatic Change, 133*, 85–100. doi:10.1007/s10584–013–1035–6

Logan, J. R., & Xu, Z. (2015). Vulnerability to hurricane damage on the U.S. Gulf Coast since 1950. *Geographical Review, 105*, 133–155. doi:10.1111/j.1931-0846.2014.12064.x

Lopes, A. M., & Machado, J. A. T. (2015). Dynamical analysis and visualization of tornadoes time series. *PLoS ONE, 10*(3), e0120260. doi:10.1371/journal.pone.0120260

Losada, C., Scaparra, M. P., & O'Hanley, J. R. (2012). Optimizing system resilience: A facility protection model with recovery time. *European Journal of Operational Research, 217*, 519–530. doi:10.1016/j.ejor.2011.09.044

Lyles, L. W., Berke, P., & Smith, G. (2013). Do planners matter? Examining factors driving incorporation of land use approaches into hazard mitigation plans. *Journal of Environmental Planning and Management, 57*, 792–811. doi:10.1080/09640568.2013.768973

Machi, L. A., & McEvoy, B. T. (2012). *The literature review: Six steps to success.* Thousand Oaks, CA: Corwin Press.

Mair, J., Ritchie, B. W., & Walters, G. (2016). Towards a research agenda for post–disaster and post–crisis recovery strategies for tourist destinations: a narrative review. *Current Issues in Tourism, 19*(1), 1. doi:10.1080/13683500.2014.932758

Makrakis, V., & Kostoulas-Makrakis, N. (2016). Bridging the qualitative–quantitative divide: Experiences from conducting a mixed methods evaluation in the RUCAS programme. *Evaluation and Program Planning, 54*, 144–151. doi:10.1016/j.evalprogplan.2015.07.008

Mancha, R. M., & Yoder, C. Y. (2015). Cultural antecedents of green behavioral intent: An environmental theory of planned behavior. *Journal of Environmental Psychology, 43*, 145–154. doi:10.1016/j.jenvp.2015.06.005

Mannakkara, S., & Wilkinson, S. (2014). Re-conceptualising "Building Back Better" to improve post-disaster recovery. *International Journal of Managing Projects in Business, 7*, 327–341. doi:10.1108/IJMPB-10-2013-0054

Marchigiani, R., Gordy, S., Cipolla, J., Adams, R. C., Evans, D. C., Stehly, C., &

Papadimos, T. J. (2013). Wind disasters: A comprehensive review of current

management strategies. *International Journal of Critical Illness & Injury Science,*

3, 130–142. doi:10.4103/2229-5151.114273

Marín, A., Bodin, Ö., Gelcich, S., & Crona, B. (2015). Social capital in post-disaster

recovery trajectories: Insights from a longitudinal study of tsunami–impacted

small–scale fisher organizations in Chile. *Global Environmental Change, 35,*

450–462. doi:10.1016/j.gloenvcha.2015.09.020

Marshall, B., Cardon, P., Poddar, A., & Fontenot, R. (2013). Does sample size matter in

qualitative research? A review of qualitative interviews in research. *Journal of*

Computer Information Systems, 54, 11–22. Retrieved from

http://www.tandfonline.com.dax.lib.unf.edu/

Marshall, C., & Rossman, G. B. (2016). *Designing qualitative research* (6th ed.).

Thousand Oaks, CA: Sage.

Marshall, M., Niehm, L., Sydnor, S., & Schrank, H. (2015). Predicting small business

demise after a natural disaster: An analysis of pre-existing conditions. *Natural*

Hazards, 79, 331–354. doi:10.1007/s11069-015-1845-0

Matzenberger, J., Hargreaves, N., Raha, D., & Dias, P. (2015). A novel approach to

assess resilience of energy systems. *International Journal of Disaster Resilience*

in the Built Environment, 6, 168–181. doi:10.1108/ijdrbe-11-2013-0044

McCarthy, J. F. (2014). Using community led development approaches to address vulnerability after disaster: Caught in a sad romance. *Global Environmental Change, 27,* 144–155. doi:10.1016/j.gloenvcha.2014.05.004

McCrae, N., Blackstock, M., & Purssell, E. (2015). Review: Eligibility criteria in systematic reviews: A methodological review. *International Journal of Nursing Studies, 52,* 1269–1276. doi:10.1016/j.ijnurstu.2015.02.002

McKnight, B., & Linnenluecke, M. K. (2016). How firm responses to natural disasters strengthen community resilience: A stakeholder–based perspective. *Organization & Environment, 29,* 290–307. doi:10.1177/1086026616629794

Medina, A. (2016). Promoting a culture of disaster preparedness. *Journal of Business Continuity & Emergency Planning, 9,* 281–290. Retrieved from http://www.henrystewartpublications.com/jbcep

Melnikov, S., Itzhaki, M., & Kagan, I. (2013). Israeli nurses' intention to report for work in an emergency or disaster. *Journal of Nursing Scholarship, 46,* 134–142. doi:10.1111/jnu.12056

Merriam, S. B., & Tisdell, E. J. (2015). *Qualitative research: A guide to design and implementation.* San Francisco, CA: Jossey-Bass.

Mika, J. (2013). Changes in weather and climate extremes: Phenomenology and empirical approaches. *Climatic Change, 121,* 15–26. doi:10.1007/s10584-013-0914-1

Mikesell, L., Bromley, E., & Khodyakov, D. (2013). Ethical community–engaged research: A literature review. *American Journal of Public Health, 103*(12), 7–14. doi:10.2105/AJPH.2012.301605

Miles, M. B., Huberman, A. M., & Saldaña, J. (2014). *Qualitative data analysis: A methods sourcebook.* Thousand Oaks, CA: Sage.

Miller, C. H., Adame, B. J., & Moore, S. D. (2013). Vested interest theory and disaster preparedness. *Disasters, 37*, 1-27. doi:10.1111/j.1467-7717.2012.01290.x

Miller, F. A., & Alvarado, K. (2005). Incorporating documents into qualitative nursing research. *Journal of Nursing Scholarship, 37*, 348-353. doi:10.1111/j.1547-5069.2005.00060.x

Miner-Romanoff, K. (2012). Interpretive and critical phenomenological crime studies: A model design. *Qualitative Report, 17*(27), 1–32. Retrieved from http://tqr.nova.edu/

Momani, N. M., & Fadil, A. S. (2013). Risk management practices in the Saudi business organizations: A case study of the city of Jeddah. *Journal of Business & Retail Management Research, 7*, 96–105. Retrieved from http://www.abrmr.com

Monllor, J., & Altay, N. (2016). Discovering opportunities in necessity: The inverse creative destruction effect. *Journal of Small Business & Enterprise Development, 23*, 274. doi:10.1108/JSBED-10-2014-0172

Morang, A. (2016). Hurricane barriers in New England and New Jersey: History and status after five decades. *Journal of Coastal Research, 317*, 181–205. doi:10.2112/jcoastres-d-14-00074.1

Morris, A., 2014. Hurricane Camille and the new politics of federal disaster relief, 1965–

1970. *Journal of Policy History, 26*, 406–426. doi:10.1017/s0898030614000189

Morrison, J. L., Titi Oladunjouye, G., & Dembry, D. (2014). An assessment of CEO

oversight of natural disaster preparedness. *International Journal of Business &*

Public Administration, 11, 66–80. Retrieved from http://www.iabpad.com

Morse, J. M. (2015). Critical analysis of strategies for determining rigor in qualitative

inquiry. *Qualitative Health Research, 25*, 1212–1222.

doi:10.1177/1049732315588501

Motter, A. E., & Campbell, D. K. (2013). Chaos at fifty. *Physics Today, 66*(5), 27–33.

doi:10.1063/PT.3.1977

Muñoz-Gómez, L. (2016). Business education and creation of awareness for disaster risk

management in Chile. *AD–Minister,* (28), 201–221.

doi:10.17230/administer.28.10

Myers, B. (1975). The Flood Disaster Protection Act of 1973. *American Business Law*

Journal, 13, 315–334. doi:10.1111/j.1744-1714.1975.tb01426.x

National Oceanic and Atmospheric Administration. (2016). *National Weather Service–*

National Hurricane Center. Retrieved from http://www.nhc.noaa.gov/

O'Daniel, P. (2013). *When the levee breaks: Memphis and the Mississippi Valley Flood*

of 1927. Charleston, SC: History Press.

Ojha, D., Gianiodis, P. T., & Manuj, I. (2013). Impact of logistical business continuity

planning on operational capabilities and financial performance. *International*

Journal of Logistics Management, 24, 180–209. doi:10.1108/ijlm-06-2012-0049

O'Reilly, M., & Parker, N. (2013). Unsatisfactory saturation: A critical exploration of the

notion of saturated sample sizes in qualitative research. *Qualitative Research, 13*,

190. doi:10.1177/1468794112446106

Owen, G. T. (2014). Evolution of a background check policy in higher education.

Qualitative Report, 19(20), 1–17. Retrieved from http://tqr.nova.edu/

Palliyaguru, R., Amaratunga, D., & Baldry, D. (2014). Constructing a holistic approach

to disaster risk reduction: The significance of focusing on vulnerability reduction.

Disasters, 38, 45–61. doi:10.1111/disa.12031

Pathak, S., & Ahmad, M. M. (2016). Flood recovery capacities of the manufacturing

SMEs from floods: A case study in Pathumthani province, Thailand. *International

Journal of Disaster Risk Reduction, 18*, 197–205. doi:10.1016/j.ijdrr.2016.07.001

Patankar, A., & Patwardhan, A. (2016). Estimating the uninsured losses due to extreme

weather events and implications for informal sector vulnerability: A case study of

Mumbai, India. *Natural Hazards, 80*, 285–310. doi:10.1007/s11069-015-1968-3

Patton, M. Q. (2015). *Qualitative research & evaluation methods*. Thousand Oaks, CA:

Sage.

Pena, A. A., Zahran, S., Underwood, A., & Weiler, S. (2014). Effect of natural disasters

on local nonprofit activity. *Growth & Change, 45*, 590-610.

doi:10.1111/grow.12056

Penning-Rowsell, E. C., & Pardoe, J. (2012). Who loses if flood risk is reduced: Should

we be concerned? *Area, 44*, 152–159. doi:10.1111/j.1475-4762.2012.01085.x

Perez, D. F., Nie, J. X., Ardern, C. I., Radhu, N., & Ritvo, P. (2013). Impact of

   participant incentives and direct and snowball sampling on survey response rate in

   an ethnically diverse community: Results from a pilot study of physical activity

   and the built environment. *Journal of Immigrant and Minority Health, 15*, 207–

   214. doi:10.1007/s10903-011-9525-y

Pérez-Nordtvedt, L., O'Brien, R., & Rasheed, A. A. (2013). What are temporary

   networks and when are they useful? *Group & Organization Management, 38*,

   392–421. doi:10.1177/1059601113485976

Perry, A. R., & Langley, C. (2013). Even with the best of intentions: Paternal

   involvement and the theory of planned behavior. *Family Process, 52*, 179–192.

   doi:10.1111/famp.12013.

Peyrovi, H., Raiesdana, N., & Mehrdad, N. (2014). Living with a heart transplant: A

   phenomenological study. *Progress in Transplantation, 24*, 234–241.

   doi:10.7182/pit2014966

Pidot, J. (2013). Deconstructing disaster. *Brigham Young University Law Review, 2*, 213–

   257. Retrieved from http://www.law2.byu.edu/lawreview

Pfaff, K. A., Baxter, P. E., Ploeg, J., & Jack, S. M. (2014). A mixed methods exploration

   of the team and organizational factors that may predict new graduate nurse

   engagement in collaborative practice. *Journal of Interprofessional Care, 28*(2),

   142–148. doi:10.3109/13561820.2013.851072

Porte, G. (2013). Who Needs Replication? *CALICO Journal, 30*(1), 10–15.

   doi:10.11139/cj. 30.1.10-15

Poussin, J. K., Wouter Botzen, W. J., & Aerts, J. C. J. H. (2015). Effectiveness of flood damage mitigation measures: Empirical evidence from French flood disasters. *Global Environmental Change, 31*, 74–84. doi:10.1016/j.gloenvcha.2014.12.007

Prazeres, A., & Lopes, E. (2013). Disaster recovery: A project–planning case study in Portugal. *Procedia Technology, 9*, 795-805. doi:10.1016/j.protcy.2013.12.088

Pressler, T. R., Yen, P., Ding, J., Liu, J., Embi, P. J., & Payne, P. O. (2012). Computational challenges and human factors influencing the design and use of clinical research participant eligibility pre–screening tools. *BMC Medical Informatics and Decision Making, 12,* 47. doi:10.1186/1472-6947-12-47

Prior, D. D., & Miller, L. M. (2012). Webethnography: Towards a typology for quality in research design. *International Journal of Market Research, 54*, 503–520. Retrieved from https://www.mrs.org.uk/ijmr_article/article/97360

Priscoli, J. D., & Stakhiv, E. (2015). Water–related disaster risk reduction (DRR) management in the United States: Floods and storm surges. *Water Policy, 17*(S1), 58-88. doi:10.2166/wp.2015.004

Prochazkova, D. (2013). Natural disasters' management and identification of priority issues for future research. *Information & Security, 29*, 127–144. Retrieved from http://procon.bg/view-volumes

Radford, L., Senkbeil, J. C., & Rockman, M. (2013). Suggestions for alternative tropical cyclone warning graphics in the USA. *Disaster Prevention and Management, 22*(3), 192–209. doi:10.1108/dpm-06-2012-0064

Randeree, K., Mahal, A., & Narwani, A. (2012). A business continuity management

maturity model for the UAE banking sector. *Business Process Management

Journal, 18*, 472–492. doi:10.1108/14637151211232650

Randolph, S. A. (2015). Emergency preparedness plan. *Workplace Health & Safety, 63*,

324. doi:10.1177/2165079915591397

Rappaport, E. N. (2014). Fatalities in the United States from Atlantic tropical cyclones:

New data and interpretation. *Bulletin of the American Meteorological Society, 95*,

341–346. doi:10.1175/bams-d-12-00074.1

Rasmussen, K. L., & Houze, R. A. (2012). A flash-flooding storm at the steep edge of

high terrain: Disaster in the Himalayas. *Bulletin of the American Meteorological

Society, 93*, 1713–1724. doi:10.1175/bams-d-11-00236.1

Reilly, R. C. (2013). Found poems, member checking and crises of representation.

Qualitative Report, 18(30), 1–18. Retrieved from http://tqr.nova.edu/

Ritchie, J., Lewis, J., McNaughton, N. C., & Ormston, R. (2013). *Qualitative research

practice: A guide for social science students and researchers*. Los Angeles, CA:

Sage.

Robinson, O. C. (2013). Sampling in Interview-Based Qualitative Research: A

Theoretical and Practical Guide. *Qualitative Research in Psychology, 11*(1), 25–

41. doi:10.1080/14780887.2013.801543

Rosenzweig, C., & Solecki, W. (2014). Hurricane Sandy and adaptation pathways in New

York: Lessons from a first-responder city. *Global Environmental Change, 28*,

395–408. doi:10.1016/j.gloenvcha.2014.05.003

Rudnick, A. (2014). A philosophical analysis of the general methodology of qualitative

research: A critical rationalist perspective. *Health Care Analysis, 22*, 245–254.

doi:10.1007/s10728-012-0212-5

Ruivo, P., Santos, V., & Oliveira, T. (2014). Data protection in services and support

roles: A qualitative research amongst ICT professionals. *Procedia Technology,

16,* 710–717. doi:10.1016/j.protcy.2014.10.020

Saarinen, J., Hambira, W. L., Atlhopheng, J., & Manwa, H. (2012). Tourism industry

reaction to climate change in Kgalagadi South District, Botswana. *Development

Southern Africa, 29*, 273–285. doi:10.1080/0376835x.2012.675697

Sadiq, A. A., & Graham, J. D. (2015). Exploring the predictors of organizational

preparedness for natural disasters. *Risk Analysis, 36,* 1040–1053.

doi:10.1111/risa.12478

Sadiq, A. A., & Tyler, J. (2016). Variations in public and private employees' perceptions

of organizational preparedness for natural disasters. *Environmental Hazards, 15,*

160–177. doi:10.1080/17477891.2016.1167010

Sahebjamnia, N., Torabi, S. A., & Mansouri, S. A. (2015). Integrated business continuity

and disaster recovery planning: Towards organizational resilience. *European

Journal of Operational Research, 242,* 261–273. doi:10.1016/j.ejor.2014.09.055

Samaddar, S., Chatterjee, R., Misra, B., & Tatano, H. (2014). Outcome–expectancy and

self–efficacy: Reasons or results of flood preparedness intention? *International

Journal of Disaster Risk Reduction, 8*, 91–99. doi:10.1016/j.ijdrr.2014.02.002

Samuel, P., Quinn Griffin, M. T., White, M., & Fitzpatrick, J. J. (2015). Crisis leadership efficacy of nurse practitioners. *Journal for Nurse Practitioners, 11*, 862–868. doi:10.1016/j.nurpra.2015.06.010

Sánchez–Fernández, J., Muñoz–Leiva, F., & Montoro-Ríos, F. J. (2012). Improving retention rate and response quality in Web–based surveys. *Computers in Human Behavior, 28*, 507–514. doi:10.1016/j.chb.2011.10.023

Sánchez–Medina, A. J., Romero–Quintero, L., & Sosa–Cabrera, S. (2014). Environmental management in small and medium–sized companies: An analysis from the perspective of the theory of planned behavior. *PLoS ONE, 9*(2), e88504. doi:10.1371/journal.pone.0088504

Sarmiento, J. P., Hoberman, G., Ilcheva, M., Asgary, A., Majano, A. M., Poggione, S., & Duran, L. R. (2015). Private sector and disaster risk reduction: The cases of Bogota, Miami, Kingston, San Jose, Santiago, and Vancouver. *International Journal of Disaster Risk Reduction, 14*, 225–237. doi:10.1016/j.ijdrr.2014.09.008

Sasirekha, V. (2013). Requirements analysis for disaster recovery plan at integral coach factory, Chennai. *Journal of Institute of Public Enterprise, 36*, 117–127. Retrieved from http://www.ipeindia.org/KenticoCMS/IPE/Journal-Home.aspx

Sawalha, I. H. S. (2014). Collaboration in crisis and emergency management: Identifying the gaps in the case of storm 'Alexa.' *Journal of Business Continuity & Emergency Planning, 7*, 312–323. Retrieved from http://www.henrystewartpublications.com/jbcep

Sawalha, I. H. S., Jraisat, L. E., & Al-Qudah, K. A. M. (2013). Crisis and disaster management in Jordanian hotels: practices and cultural considerations. *Disaster Prevention and Management, 22*, 210-228. doi:10.1108/dpm-09-2012-0101

Schrank, H., Marshall, M., Hall-Phillips, A., Wiatt, R., & Jones, N. (2013). Small–business demise and recovery after Katrina: Rate of survival and demise. *Natural Hazards, 65*, 2353-2374. doi:10.1007/s11069-012-0480-2

Seara, T., Clay, P. M., & Colburn, L. L. (2016). Perceived adaptive capacity and natural disasters: A fisheries case study. *Global Environmental Change, 38*, 49–57. doi:10.1016/j.gloenvcha.2016.01.006

Shepherd, D. A., & Williams, T. A. (2014). Local venturing as compassion organizing in the aftermath of a natural disaster: The role of localness and community in reducing suffering. *Journal of Management Studies, 51*, 952–994. doi:10.1111/joms.12084

Shockley, G. (2015). The international handbook on social innovation: Collective action, social learning and transdisciplinary research (F. Moulaert, D. MacCallum, A. Mehmood, & A. Hamdouch, Eds.). 2013. Cheltenham, U.K. and Northampton, Massachusetts: Edward Elgar [Book review]. *Journal of Regional Science, 55*, 152–154. doi:10.1111/jors.12182

Shreve, C. M., & Kelman, I. (2014). Does mitigation save? Reviewing cost-benefit analyses of disaster risk reduction. *International Journal of Disaster Risk Reduction, 10*, 213–235. doi:10.1016/j.ijdrr.2014.08.004

Siebeneck, L. K., Lindell, M. K., Prater, C. S., Wu, H.-C., & Huang, S.-K. (2012).

Evacuees' reentry concerns and experiences in the aftermath of Hurricane Ike.

Natural Hazards, 65, 2267–2286. doi:10.1007/s11069-012-0474-0

Sinkovics, R., & Alfoldi, E. (2012). Progressive focusing and trustworthiness in

qualitative research. *Management International Review, 52*, 817–845.

doi:10.1007/s11575-012-0140-5

Sivacek, J., & Crano, W. D. (1982). Vested interest as a moderator of attitude–behavior

consistency. *Journal of Personality and Social Psychology, 43*, 210–221.

doi:10.1037/0022–3514.43.2.210

Skiba, J. M., & Disch, W. B. (2014). A phenomenological study of the barriers and

challenges facing insurance fraud investigators. *Journal of Insurance Regulation,

33*, 87–114. Retrieved from http://www.naic.org/prod_serv_jir.htm

Smith, A. M., & O'Sullivan, T. (2012). Environmentally responsible behaviour in the

workplace: An internal social marketing approach. *Journal of Marketing

Management, 28*, 469–493. doi:10.1080/0267257x.2012.658837

Smith, D. J., & Sutter, D. (2013). Response and recovery after the Joplin Tornado.

Independent Review, 18, 165–188. Retrieved from

http://www.independent.org/review.html

Smith, J. K., & Lougee, B. A. (2014). The appraiser's role in calculating casualty loss

deductions from natural disasters. *Appraisal Journal, 82*, 27–36. Retrieved from

http://www.appraisalinstitute.org/publications/periodicals/taj/default.asp

Smith, S. J., & Bond, T. C. (2014). Two hundred fifty years of aerosols and climate: The

end of the age of aerosols. *Atmospheric Chemistry & Physics, 14*, 537–549.

doi:10.5194/acp-14-537-2014

Sniehotta, F. F., Presseau, J., & Araújo–Soares, V. (2014). Time to retire the theory of

planned behaviour. *Health Psychology Review, 8*, 1–7.

doi:10.1080/17437199.2013.869710

Snyder, C. (2012). A case study of a case study: Analysis of a robust qualitative research

methodology. *Qualitative Report, 17*(13), 1–21. Retrieved from

http://tqr.nova.edu/

Sonenshein, S., DeCelles, K. A. & Dutton, J. E. (2014). It's not easy being green: The

role of self–evaluations in explaining support of environmental issues. *Academy

of Management Journal, 57*, 7–37. doi:10.5465/amj.2010.0445

Stanimirovic, D., & Vintar, M. (2015). The role of information and communication

technology in the transformation of the healthcare business model: A case study

of Slovenia. *Health Information Management Journal, 44*(2), 20–32.

doi:10.12826/18333575.2014.0015

Stake, R. E. (2010). *Qualitative research: Studying how things work.* New York, NY:

Guilford Press.

Strauss, A. & Corbin, J. (2015). *Basics of qualitative research: Techniques and

procedures for developing grounded theory.* Thousand Oaks, CA: Sage.

Steelman, T. A., & McCaffrey, S. (2013). Best practices in risk and crisis

communication: Implications for natural hazards management. *Natural Hazards,*

65, 683–705. doi:10.1007/s11069-012-0386-z

Stewart, S. R. (2013). Atlantic hurricanes 2012: Northeastern United States devastated by

Sandy. *Weatherwise, 66*(3), 28–39. doi:10.1080/00431672.2013.781846

Strang, D. K. (2014). Assessing natural disaster survivor evacuation attitudes to inform

social policy. *International Journal of Society & Social Policy, 34*, 485–510.

doi:10.1108/ijssp-04-2013-0040

Strause, L. (2013). Patient-first approach to improve oncology clinical trials. *Applied*

Clinical Trials, 22(3), 26–31. Retrieved from

http://www.appliedclinicaltrialsonline.com

Su, C.-C, & Ni, F.-Y. (2013). Budgetary participation and slack on the theory of planned

behavior. *International Journal of Organizational Innovation, 5*(4), 91–99.

Retrieved from http://www.ijoi-online.org/

Taber, K. S. (2012). Prioritizing paradigms, mixing methods, and characterizing the

'qualitative' in educational research. *Teacher Development, 16*, 125–138.

doi:10.1080/13664530.2012.674294

Taneja, S., Pryor, M. G., Humphreys, J. H., & Singleton, L. P. (2013). Strategic

management in an era of paradigmatic chaos: Lessons for managers. *International*

Journal of Management, 30, 112–126. Retrieved from http://www.theijm.com/

Taramelli, A., Valentini, E., & Sterlacchini, S. (2015). A GIS–based approach for hurricane hazard and vulnerability assessment in the Cayman Islands. *Ocean & Coastal Management, 108*, 116–130. doi:10.1016/j.ocecoaman.2014.07.021

Taubman, M. T., Leaf, R. B., McEachin, J. J., Papovich, S., & Leaf, J. B. (2013). A comparison of data collection techniques used with discrete trial teaching. *Research in Autism Spectrum Disorders, 7*, 1026–1034. doi:10.1016/j.rasd.2013.05.002

Taylor, A., Bruine de Bruin, W., & Dessai, S. (2014). Climate change beliefs and perceptions of weather–related changes in the United Kingdom. *Risk Analysis: An International Journal, 34*, 1995–2004. doi:10.1111/risa.12234

Teng, Y., Wu, K., & Liu, H. (2015). Integrating altruism and the theory of planned behavior to predict patronage intention of a green hotel. *Journal of Hospitality & Tourism Research, 39*, 299–315. doi:10.1177/1096348012471383

Thomas, W. I., & Znaniecki, F. (1918). *The Polish peasant in Europe and America.* Boston, MA: Badger.

Tiwari, S., Dumka, U. C., Hopke, P. K., Tunved, P., Srivastava, A. K., Bisht, D. S., & Chakrabarty, R. K. (2016). Atmospheric heating due to black carbon aerosol during the summer monsoon period over Ballia: A rural environment over Indo–Gangetic Plain. *Atmospheric Research, 178–179*, 393–400. doi:10.1016/j.atmosres.2016.04.008

Torabi, S. A., Rezaei Soufi, H., & Sahebjamnia, N. (2014). A new framework for

business impact analysis in business continuity management (with a case study).

Safety Science, 68, 309–323. doi:10.1016/j.ssci.2014.04.017

Torres, H., & Alsharif, K. (2016). Reflecting on resilience in Broward County, Florida: A

newspaper content analysis about Hurricane Wilma recovery. *International

Journal of Disaster Risk Reduction, 19*, 36–46. doi:10.1016/j.ijdrr.2016.08.007

Trumbo, C., Meyer, M. A., Marlatt, H., Peek, L., & Morrissey, B. (2013). An assessment

of change in risk perception and optimistic bias for hurricanes among Gulf Coast

residents. *Risk Analysis, 34*, 1013–1024. doi:10.1111/risa.12149

Tsang, E. W. K. (2013). Generalizing from research findings: The merits of case studies.

International Journal of Management Reviews, 16, 369–383.

doi:10.1111/ijmr.12024

United Nations Office for Disaster Risk Reduction. (2013). *Global Assessment Report.*

Retrieved from https://www.unisdr.org/we/inform/publications/33013

Unluer, S. (2012). Being an insider researcher while conducting case study research.

Qualitative Report, 17(29), 1–14. Retrieved from

http://www.nova.edu/ssss/QR/index.html

U.S. Small Business Administration. (2014). *Frequently asked questions.* Santa

Ana:Author. Retrieved from

https://www.sba.gov/sites/default/files/FAQ_March_2014_0.pdf

U.S. Small Business Administration. (2016). Disaster planning. Retrieved from

    https://www.sba.gov/managing-business/running–business/emergency–

    preparedness/disaster-planning

Uță, D. S., & Popescu, C. (2013). Shaping attitudes: Analysis of existing models.

    Economic Insights: Trends & Challenges, 65(3), 61–71. Retrieved from

    http://www.upg-bulletin-se.ro

Van der Vegt, G. S., Essens, P., Wahlström, M., & George, G. (2015). Managing risk and

    resilience. *Academy of Management Journal, 58*, 971–980.

    doi:10.5465/amj.2015.4004

Van Wijk, E. (2014). Recruitment and retention of vulnerable populations: Lessons

    learned from a longitudinal qualitative study. *Qualitative Report, 19*, 28–49.

    Retrieved from http://tqr.nova.edu/

Venkatesh, V., Brown, S. A., & Bala, H. (2013). Bridging the qualitative-quantitative

    divide: Guidelines for conducting mixed methods research in information

    systems. *MIS Quarterly, 37*, 21–54. Retrieved from http://www.misq.org

Villarini, G., Goska, R., Smith, J. A., & Vecchi, G. A. (2014). North Atlantic tropical

    cyclones and U.S. flooding. *Bulletin of the American Meteorological Society, 95*,

    1381–1388. doi:10.1175/bams-d-13-00060.1

Vinayagamoorthy, A. (2014). Micro insurance: A conceptual study. *International*

    Journal of Trade & Global Business Perspectives, 3, 1331–1335. Retrieved from

    http://pezzottaitejournals.net/index.php/IJTGBP

Vlassopoulos, C. A. (2012). Competing definition of climate change and the post–Kyoto

negotiations. *International Journal of Climate Change Strategies and

Management, 4*, 104–118. doi:10.1108/17568691211200245

Wai, L. C., & Wongsurawat, W. (2013). Crisis management: Western Digital's 46-day

recovery from the 2011 flood disaster in Thailand. *Strategy & Leadership, 41*,

34–38. doi:10.1108/10878571311290061

Walker, B., & Redmond, J. (2014). Changing the environmental behavior of small

business owners: The business case. *Australian Journal of Environmental

Education, 30*, 254–268. doi:10.1017/aee.2015.6

Walker, J. L. (2012). The use of saturation in qualitative research. *Canadian Journal of

Cardiovascular Nursing, 22*(2), 37–41. Retrieved from http://www.cccn.ca

Wallace, Z. C., Keys-Mathews, L., & Hill, A. A. (2015). The role of experience in

defining tornado risk perceptions: A case from the 27 April 2011 outbreak in rural

Alabama. *Southeastern Geographer, 55*, 400–416. doi:10.1353/sgo.2015.0035

Wang, J., & Ritchie, B. W. (2012). Understanding accommodation managers' crisis

planning intention: An application of the theory of planned behaviour. *Tourism

Management, 33*, 1057–1067. doi:10.1016/j.tourman.2011.12.006

Wasileski, G., Rodríguez, H., & Diaz, W. (2011). Business closure and relocation: A

comparative analysis of the Loma Prieta earthquake and Hurricane Andrew.

Disasters, 35, 102–129. doi:10.1111/j.1467-7717.2010.01195.x

Webb, A. (2015). Research interviews in the scholarship of teaching and learning. *Transformative Dialogues: Teaching & Learning Journal, 8*, 1–8. Retrieved from http://www.kwantlen.ca/

Webber, R., & Jones, K. (2013). Rebuilding communities after natural disasters: The 2009 bushfires in southeastern Australia. *Journal of Social Service Research, 39*, 253–268. doi:10.1080/01488376.2012.754196

Wedawatta, G., Ingirige, B., & Proverbs, D. (2013). Small businesses and flood impacts: the case of the 2009 flood event in Cockermouth. *Journal of Flood Risk Management, 7*, 42–53. doi:10.1111/jfr3.12031

Welle, P. G. (2012). Risk and precautionary approaches to climate change: Conceptual and empirical lessons from the insurance industry. *Journal of Management Policy & Practice, 13*(4), 88–101. Retrieved from http://www.na–businesspress.com

Wharton, M. P. (2012). The Johnstown Flood of 1889. *Journalism History, 38*, 23–33. Retrieved from http://www.unlv.edu/Colleges/Greenspun/Journalism_History

White, D. E., Oelke, N. D., & Friesen, S. (2012). Management of a large qualitative data set: Establishing trustworthiness of the data. *International Journal of Qualitative Methods, 11*, 244–258. Retrieved from https://ejournals.library.ualberta.ca/index.php/IJQM/

Whitman, Z., Stevenson, J., Kachali, H., Seville, E., Vargo, J., & Wilson, T. (2014). Organisational resilience following the Darfield earthquake of 2010. *Disasters, 38*, 148–177. doi:10.1111/disa.12036

Wibbenmeyer, M. J., Hand, M. S., Calkin, D. E., Venn, T. J., & Thompson, M. P. (2013).

    Risk preferences in strategic wildfire decision making: A choice experiment with

    U.S. wildfire managers. *Risk Analysis: An International Journal, 33*, 1021–1037.

    doi:10.1111/j.1539-6924.2012.01894.x

Williams, B. (2015). How to evaluate qualitative research. *American Nurse Today,*

    10(11), 31–38. Retrieved from http://americannursetoday.com

Williams, S., & Schaefer, A. (2013). Small and medium–sized enterprises and

    sustainability: Managers' values and engagement with environmental and climate

    change issues. *Business Strategy & the Environment, 22*(3), 173–186.

    doi:10.1002/bse.1740

Woods, M., Paulus, T., Atkins, D. P., & Macklin, R. (2015). Advancing qualitative

    research using qualitative data analysis software (QDAS)? Reviewing potential

    versus practice in published studies using ATLAS.ti and NVivo, 1994–2013.

    Social Science Computer Review. Advance online publication.

    doi:10.1177/0894439315596311

Xiao, Y., & Drucker, J. (2013). Does economic diversity enhance regional disaster

    resilience? *Journal of the American Planning Association, 79*, 148–160.

    doi:10.1080/01944363.2013.882125

Xiao, Y., & Feser, E. (2013). The unemployment impact of the 1993 US Midwest flood:

    A quasi–experimental structural break point analysis. *Environmental Hazards,*

    13(2), 93–113. doi:10.1080/17477891.2013.777892

Xiao, Y., & Nilawar, U. (2013). Winners and losers: Analyzing post–disaster spatial economic demand shift. *Disasters, 37*, 646–668. doi:10.1111/disa.12025

Xiao, Y., & Peacock, W. G. (2014). Do Hazard Mitigation and Preparedness Reduce Physical Damage to Businesses in Disasters? Critical Role of Business Disaster Planning. *Natural Hazards Review, 15(3)*, 04014007. doi:10.1061/(asce)nh.1527-6996.0000137

Xin, H., Karamehic-Muratovic, A., & Cluphf, D. (2016). A Bosnian refugee community's hidden capacity in preparation for a natural disaster in the United States. *Global Journal of Health Education and Promotion, 17, 53–71.* doi:10.18666/gjhep-2016-v17-i1-6131

Yang, L., Kajitani, Y., Tatano, H., & Jiang, X. (2016). A methodology for estimating business interruption loss caused by flood disasters: Insights from business surveys after Tokai Heavy Rain in Japan. *Natural Hazards, 84*, 411–430. doi:10.1007/s11069-016-2534-3

Yang, T.-M., & Wu, Y.-J. (2014). Exploring the determinants of cross-boundary information sharing in the public sector: An e-government case study in Taiwan. *Journal of Information Science, 40*, 649–668. doi:10.1177/0165551514538742

Yilmaz, K. (2013). Comparison of quantitative and qualitative research traditions: Epistemological, theoretical, and methodological differences. *European Journal of Education, 48*, 311–325. doi:10.1111/ejed.12014

Yin, R. K. (2012). *Applications of case study research.* Thousand Oaks, CA: Sage.

Yin, R. K. (2014). *Case study research: Design and methods.* Los Angeles, CA: Sage.

Yu, L., Yuan, Z., Zhang, Y., & Liu, C. (2013). Using evidence–based paradigm to iteratively acquire the overall picture of primary research question. *Journal of Software, 8*, 1634–1641. doi:10.4304/jsw.8.7.1634–1641

Zolin, R., & Kropp, F. (2007). How surviving businesses respond during and after a major disaster. *Journal of Business Continuity & Emergency Planning, 1*, 183–199. Retrieved from http://www.henrystewartpublications.com/jbcep

Zou, X., Weng, F., Zhang, B., Lin, L., Qin, Z., & Tallapragada, V. (2013). Impacts of assimilation of ATMS data in HWRF on track and intensity forecasts of 2012 four landfall hurricanes. *Journal of Geophysical Research: Atmospheres, 118*, 11,558–11,576. doi:10.1002/2013JD020

Zissimopoulos, M., & Karoly, L. A. (2010). Employment and self-employment in the wake of Hurricane Katrina. *Demography, 47*, 345–367. Retrieved from http://www.springer.com/social+sciences/population+studies/journal/13524